TABLE OF CONTENTS

CHAPTER 1   4
INTRODUCTION

     I. Elements of a Statement
     II. Recorded Statement Format
     III. Written Statement Format
     IV. Principles of Interviewing
     V. Interviewing Do's
     VI. Interviewing Don'ts
     VII. Getting Started
     VIII. Recording Devices
     IX. Duplicating Statement for Client or Evidence File

CHAPTER 2   19
WORKERS' COMPENSATION STATEMENTS

     Workers' Compensation General Fact Statement - Outline

     Supplemental Questions for Specific Injuries

        Back Injury
        Head Injury
        Heart Attack
        Heat Stroke
        Assaults
        Eye Injury
        Dependent Claims
        Dermatitis
        Going & Coming Claims
        Carpel Tunnel Syndrome
        Knee Injury
        Long shore and Harbor Workers Claims

     Workers' Compensation Supplemental Witness Questions

        Witness Statement - eyewitness to injury
        Witness Statement - unwitnessed injury
        Foreman/Supervisor Statement - eye witness
        Foreman/Supervisor Statement - unwitnessed injury

CHAPTER 3 AUTOMOBILE LIABILITY	51

    Automobile General Fact Statement - Outline
    Permissive Use Statement
    Permissive Use Statement (Streamline Version)
    Police Officer's Statement
    Statement of Insured in Guest Case
    Guest's Exonerating Statement
    Minor Bodily Injury Statement
    PIP Statement from Insured
    PIP Statement from Driver

CHAPTER 4 AUTO THEFT	70

  Automobile Theft General Fact Statement-Outline

CHAPTER 5 GENERAL LIABILITY	76

    Slip/Fall Statement
    Dog Bite Statement

CHAPTER 6 HOMEOWNER THEFT/BURGLARY	83

    Property Theft Statement

CHAPTER 7 FIRE STATEMENTS QUESTIONS	88

    Statement from Discover(s) of Fire
    Statement from Insured/Owner/Landlord/Tenant(s) and Occupant(s)
    Statement from Neighbors
    Statement from Firemen, Fire Marshall & Police Officers
    Statement from Insurance Agent

CHAPTER 8 CASE STUDIES	95

    Premium Fraud
    Auto Repair Scheme
    Brake Checking

Slip and Fall
Staged Pedestrian Accident
Apartment Fire
Security Guard Shooting

CHAPTER 9   136
RELEASES AND AFFIUDAVITS

Interview/photograph minor child
Medial release in Spanish
No insurance affidavit
General release
HIIPA

CHAPTER 10   143
STATUTES FOR STATEMENTS

CHAPTER 1 INTRODUCTION

I. ELEMENTS OF A STATEMENT

It's very common to conduct interviews and secure written or recorded statements when conducting an investigation. These statements may be crucial in providing corroborative supporting evidence or dismissive deceptive evidence showing the subject was untruthful. Statements are taken to document a subject's knowledge or facts about a matter and to memorialize this information while it's still fresh in their mind. Within the statement we will want to get as much personal information about the subject as possible keeping in mind that this case may go on for a year, two or several for that matter and being able to locate the witness at a later time will depend on the amount of information you secure about them now. So getting what we call identifying information about the witness as well as other family members will make locating them a lot easier when the time comes to produce them as a witness.

We know that statistically, about twenty-five percent of the nation's population moves every year for various reasons so the more information you can get about a subject without being too over bearing will prove well worth it if your witness is one of those that moved.

Interviewing is an art that you will get better at overtime. Confidence in your ability to understand what the witness is telling you is critical. If they are describing a complicated matter have them draw it out, show you pictures or even take you there. Don't move on in the statement until you understand every detail of what has already been said. Listen carefully as follow-up questions will clarify any uncertainty and are critical to getting those details that can be investigated afterwards to corroborate or pierce the falsehood of the witness' statement. You can never get too many details and through these details we obtain additional leads to pursue and verify.

Too often you hear investigators report, that the subject appeared <u>untruthful</u> because they neglected eye contact, fidgeted in their seat or sat with their arms or legs crossed. There are also verbal indicators where the subject asks you to repeat the question, there is a delayed response or the answer is overly specific or overly vague. While these are often indicators of lying, only facts that come from the subject's statement, proven and disproven will provide the documentation to verify the legitimacy of the statement.

If I hook you up to a lie detection machine, will the information it provides be accurate? The answer is simply YES. A lie detection machine does exactly what it is designed to do, read a person's heartbeat, record movement and perspiration. The art in the "Lie Detection", used ONLY as a TOOL, is in the operator's ability to establish reliable data. And regardless of the information, it can still only be used as a tool and the results are not admissible in court. Many Claims Investigators, especially those using this book will be new to the business and must understand that we don't rely on lie detection techniques to draw conclusions; we use them to keep probing and ask more questions.

I always act as if I believe their story to encourage more details, but if they are not coming, I ask questions that would seem to support their story if it were true to get those details that may be missing. As you get deeper in questioning and it is obvious to both parties that the statement is no longer making any sense, offer the person the opportunity to go off the record. Say to them, I think we both know that this is not going very well. I think it's time before you get in too deep to set the record straight. Nobody wants to commit insurance fraud over a simple accident. Let them know you will turn the recorder back on and get the real story and if they have to, have them withdrawal the claim.

Some of the most believable liars are criminals and drug addicts. Both are so used to covering up their tracks that lies come natural and they can be incredibly convincing. I just keep them talking so that I have as many details as possible. You may have heard the saying "Loose Lips Sink Ships" well that's exactly the principle behind getting as much information as possible. .

Recently I investigated an auto theft and the owner advised that her home had also been broken into. Apparently the thief broke into the house and stole the car keys. The owner of the car was hospitalized at the time and was relying on details reported to her by her son. The car had subsequently been involved in an accident near an office park and after the crash the car thief fled the area on foot. Footage of the thief was caught on an area businesses security camera. The person in the video looked very similar to the car owner's son. The image was grainy and distant, but the tall slender short dark haired twenty-year-old subject seemed to fit him perfect. He also had a somewhat unique gait which seemed to be noted in the footage.

Prior to interviewing the subject, I learned he had a history of drug abuse with his drug of preference the very addictive prescription pain killer known as Oxycotin. When I met the tall slender male he was wearing penny loafers, designer jeans and a sports coat. He began the introduction with a long story about his history and how my difficulty in contacting him was due to working with his father in Daytona Beach and going to school at night. During the interview he reported that he had been at the hospital with his mother for three days over the time period the house was burglarized. He had gone back and forth with a friend twice to get things for his mother but at the time the car theft and accident he was at the hospital. As I let him speak for almost two hours, he provided such incredible details. He advised that on the date of the accident at 3:00 a.m. which was actually five hours before the accident, he was returning to the hospital from one of those trips home to get some clothes and personal items for his hospitalized mother. He reported that he was driven to downtown Orlando by his friend Josh. At around 3:00 a.m. they stopped at a 7/11 on Orange Avenue near ORMC to purchase some items before actually arriving at the hospital. Later that same morning, he stated that he walked to that same 7/11 around 8:00 a.m. He stated that the same clerk who waited on him at 3:00 a.m. waited on him again at 8:00 a.m. He described the worker as a dark skinned "Indian" female in her 20's. He stated that he was certain she would remember him because, he was dressed in "Stewie" pajamas (from Family Guy), wearing a black jacket and high leather boots. He also stated that during his first visit there the young woman stopped him from leaving when he forgot to pick up the cigarettes he purchased. During the second visit she asked if he was still having a rough day. He also stated that when he returned, they had just served his mom pancakes and the hospital serves breakfast at 8:00 a.m. His mother who was listening in agreed with everything he was saying. Based on the subject's statement he could not have crashed the car in Sanford at 8:00 a.m. and also be in south Orlando at 8:00 a.m.

I determined that there are two 7/11 stores within walking distance of ORMC. One located at 1823 South Orange Avenue (referred to as the Kaley Store) and one located at 902 Gore Street. I determined that neither store had a female in her 20's working a third shift. Furthermore, the third shift girl would not have still been at the store by 8:00 a.m. The witness also stated that the clerk was a darker skinned Indian or Latin and neither store had any personnel that fit that description working the overnight shift. The managers in both stores agreed to review the video footage for that day and a follow-up call advised me that the subject was not observed in their store over the time period stated.

Later that evening I tried to call the subject to clarify if I had the right area or the right stores. I persisted with several more calls to the witnesses advising that what he had told me did not check out. He never responded.

Always go out and check the information provided in any statement. Talk to all of the people mentioned in the statement or visit any place they said they visited to see if it can be verified. You will find that through thoroughness you will become a successful investigator. There will be those that stop short of verifying all information or feel the drive to visit a location is not worthwhile. It's through these little acts of disregard or apathy that separates a good investigator from a bad one. As investigators, a large part of our work is investigating incidents or accidents. Incidents that occur at work to employees are investigated by the employers' agents, and companies that insure employers and their employees. Employers are expected to maintain safe environments for their workers. When a worker is required to clean the windows from the outside of a high-rise building, there are security procedures the workers follow to protect them from any workplace dangers. For instance they are required to wear tethers or body harnesses in case of a fall. Most of us can relate to having auto insurance to cover any injury in an automobile accident. Our auto coverage provides protection in case we are injured in the accident or whether we injury someone else. The coverage also reimburses us for the damage to our cars or the cars we struck in the accident. It also covers any other property we may have damaged if perhaps for example we ran into a fence or building that needs to be repaired. In my earlier statements, I mentioned that law enforcement agencies handle criminal matters however, when these incidents occur many times, a private party is brought into the matter. For instance, if a person is shot by an assailant during a robbery the Police will investigate the matter but so will the insurance company that insures the business and their employees. Since this shooting or incident occurred at work and the employee's injuries would be covered by their workplace insurance, the insurance company's representative would look into the matter for clarification of what happened. The worker at the same time may have been seriously injured and may seek his own legal representation to assure his best interests are protected. He may not be able to go back to work and may have a permanent personal injury or permanent disability. An investigator may be hired by the injured person's attorney to secure all of the facts of the incident.

So in any incident or accident, there may be law enforcement investigators working a case and private investigators representing different parties or sides of the matter. The investigators have different responsibilities and objectives. The Law Enforcement Officer is looking to apprehend the assailant. The Private Investigator hired by the employer or their insurance company is going to look into the workplace environment and the security provided to protect the worker from harm. The PI will start to show that the workplace did have the security required to protect the worker based on information they were able to collect during the investigation. Issues concerning crime in the immediate area as well as specific incidents of a similar nature occurring at the employer's specific location will all be collected.

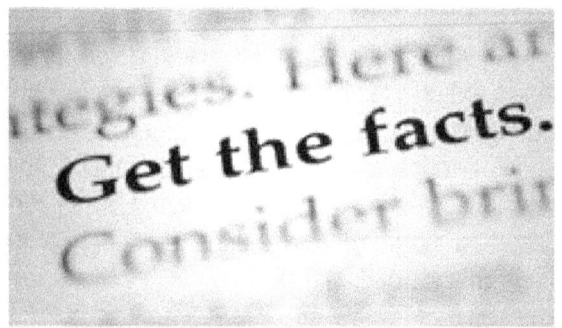

OBJECTIVE

The topic of investigating Incidents and accidents covers a very broad spectrum. Many incidents and accidents occur while we are at work. Businesses need to know and understand the risks faced by their employees and the best way to understand them is to investigate the critical components of who, what, where, when, why, and how.

A good statement taker will need to pull details from the witness's memory. There will be details that they don't realize are important. Before going out, make sure you have a clear understanding of your objective. You can't conduct a thorough interview if all you ask is what happened.

Knowing and understanding the reason for the statement is key to even knowing what questions to ask. A client may ask for a statement simply to document their file. However, their purpose may be to determine liability, subrogation possibilities or to inquire about a possible pre-existing medical condition. There can be a million reasons why you are securing the statement and in order to do well in each instance you need to prepare. Always have a guide to follow as well as additional specific questions that may be relative to the issue and need to be answered. Always have a notepad to jot down questions that come to you while the witness is talking. So, before going out, make sure you have a clear understanding of your objective. You can't conduct a thorough interview if all you ask is what happened, who was injured, and who or what was responsible.

The following are a few examples of why one would be taking a statement in a particular type of claim.

Auto:

Liability--Subrogation--Uninsured Motorist--Wrongful Death--PIP

Workers' Compensation:

Compensability--Subrogation--Pre-exiting Condition

Slip and Fall:

Liability and Subrogation

Medical Malpractice:

Liability

Food Poisoning:

Liability

Fire and Arson:

Motive (assets)--Point of Origin--Flammables--Property Damage

Auto Theft:

Keys--Financial, Mechanical Problems

Theft:

Property Loss--Forced Entry--Property Damage Loss List

PREPARATION

Review your assignment and locate a good "base" outline appropriate to the type of claim. Have a note pad and diagram sheet available. Make your own list of questions as well.

All Statements will follow the basic format with an INTRODUCTION; BODY OF STATEMENT (questions); and a CLOSING (refer to following page for example).

PLAN AND CONTROL

Carefully plan the conversation, briefly outline your approach. Take notes, during the conversation. Listen to the interviewee's responses. Their responses should prompt additional clarification questions or follow-up questions referred to second and third tier questions. Remember, anyone listening to or reading the transcription from a recorded statement should have enough information to understand the incident or accident being explored.

INFORMALITY

Remember to use an informal positive approach. If you want a person to be your friend, treat him as if he is your friend; if you want a recorded statement, treat him as if he <u>will</u> give you one.

REVIEW

Review the claim and have all known facts well fixed in your mind.

COURTESY

Remember -- courtesy is essential.

II. RECORDED STATEMENT FORMAT

(Turn Recorder On)

Today's date is <u>(date)</u>. My name is <u>(your name)</u>. I am employed with <u>(Agency Name)</u>, and I am representing (name of Client Company). I am at (the location where you are taking statement).

I am interviewing (name of subject) who was (involved in the accident/incident, witnessed, etc.). (Name of person) Are you aware that I am recording our conversation? (Response) Do I have your permission to do so? (Response)

BODY OF STATEMENT

Depending on type of statement, refer to statement outlines and your own prepared notes and questions. Address the specific concerns of the client, such as any special questions indicated on the assignment sheet that must be covered. Be certain that you fully cover and understand how the incident or accident occurred. This should be a relaxed conversation so put your interviewee and yourself at ease. Don't be afraid to ask questions out of order. If a question comes to mind ask it. You can rarely ask too many questions.

CLOSING

Ask:

Is there anything else you would like to add or clarify in this statement before I conclude the recording? (Response). (If response is no) . . . If there is nothing else, I will conclude this statement.

(Subject's name) were you aware that I was recording our conversation? (If the response is no, proceed with closing; If the response is yes, let the subject explain and ask follow up questions if necessary. Once you are through, repeat this statement again before proceeding.) (Subject's Name) Were you aware I was recording our conversation? (Response)) Did I have your permission to do so? (Response) (Subject's Name) Was everything you told me true and correct to the best of your knowledge and belief? (Response) Would you please statement your name for the final time. My name is (Your Name). Thank you for voluntarily giving this statement. (Turn Recorder Off).

NOTE

When taking a statement, avoid turning the recorder off once statement is started. If you do, you must say why the recorder is being turned off. When you turn it back on, you need to state that you are continuing with the recording and identify person and self again.

III. WRITTEN STATEMENT FORMAT

The most obvious difference between the two will be the means in which the statement is taken. Be ready to write for an extended length of time so find a comfortable writing position at a desk or table.

Make certain you are using carbonless, three part lined statement paper. This paper is available through a specialty office supply retailer. The top original white copy will be sent to the client with your report. The next yellow copy will be stapled to your notes and become part of the office file and the third part should be handed to the person whom the statement was taken from. If you do not have this specialty paper, using a piece of carbon paper inserted between the pages of an ordinary writing pad will create the same copies.

Fill in date, place of taking, and page number of statement in upper right hand corner.

The written statement should be taken as if the person wrote it themselves. You should however write the statement so that all vital questions are answered. Also, by the investigator writing the statement, the handwriting should be legible. The written statement should a continuous narrative without any paragraphs or blank spaces. If you make a mistake both parties should initial the correction. Below is an example of how the statement should be written.

Example:

My name is Veronica M. Brown and I am here today this 10th day of June with James Corn of Claims Resource Incorporated. We are here today in regards to the <u>automobile accident, slip and fall, stolen property, etc.</u>, which occurred on (<u>date</u>) and (<u>location</u>). I am a 25 years old white female, born on July 7, 1965. I currently reside at 1276 Deer Lake Circle, Apopka, Florida 32712. My telephone number is 904-896-4629. I am married to Tim Brown who presently works for All American Gym as the manager (additional witness identification information). On the afternoon at approximately 2:30 p.m., I was driving home from having just picked my husband up from work. I was driving our 1993 blue Plymouth Voyager while my husband was seated on the passenger's side when he yelled look out! Just then I slammed on my breaks and skidded approximately 20 feet. We were both wearing our seat belts and I was only driving at approximately 45 mph so we stopped in time. The road was dry and it was a clear day. Since my husband was on the passenger side and staring out the passenger side window, he noticed a stampeding bull headed right for the road in from of us. We were driving on Old Winter Garden road heading south and my husband was starring east. The guy behind us had been tail gating me for about 5 miles ever since I left the gym. At about five miles on Old Winter Garden Road, the area gets real rural and I guess he felt it was a good place to pass. The guy who was passing me must have been looking for any oncoming cars because he sure didn't see that bull coming etc...

Remember, as this hypothetical example exhibits, each line should be continuous without any large spaces. This will prevent any room to alter or add information to the final statement that was not intended to be part of the statement. Whenever any corrections or error is made, be sure to have the interviewee initial the corrections. Number each page by using "Page 1 of 3; Page 2 of 3; Page 3 of 3", etc.

CLOSING

Have the interviewee initial each page.

Ask the subject whether there is anything else they would like to say with regards to this incident. Write exactly what they say. If they have nothing else to say, close with the following final statement and the interviewee's signature.

"I have read the above statement of _____ pages and it is true and correct to the best of my knowledge and belief." X_____(Signature of Interviewee)

Detach the last (pink) copy of the three part statement paper and provide the interviewee with a complete copy of his written statement.

IV. PRINCIPLES OF INTERVIEWING

INTERVIEWING	is a <u>specialized</u> way of asking questions.
INTERVIEWING	is the art of extracting the <u>maximum</u> amount of <u>truthful</u> information from an individual.
INTERVIEW	is the questioning of a person who is believed to possess knowledge that is of official interest to the investigator.

An <u>INTERVIEW</u> is conducted for the purpose of gaining information that may establish the facts of an accident or incident and that may provide the investigator with leads which will further substantiate the validity of the claim.

In an <u>INTERVIEW</u> (claimants, witnesses, employers, supervisors, co-workers, etc.) the interviewee usually gives his account of the accident/incident in his own words and in his own way.

In an <u>INTERVIEW</u>, a specialized way and/or technique is used in asking questions.

WITNESS	one who has <u>seen</u> or <u>knows</u> something concerning the incident under investigation and is competent of discussing it.

WHO? WHAT? WHEN? WHERE? WHY? HOW?	6 basic questions which must be exploited to the maximum in every interview.

V. INTERVIEWING DO'S

1. DO provide a suitable place for the interview.
2. DO fix the time for the interview, if possible.
3. DO have the witness conform to your arrangements, if possible.
4. DO show some consideration for the witness, once he indicates that he is cooperating.
5. DO seat the witness and place him at ease.
6. DO seat the witness so that the light, if any, falls on him is possible.
7. DO show courtesy and politeness toward the ordinary witness.
8. DO create a motive for the witness to provide you with information.
9. DO assure the witness of protection of unnecessary disclosure.
10. DO distinguish between a witness and a bias witness.
11. DO seek to identify the witness's interest with yours, in the mind of the witness.
12. DO seek to win the confidence of the witness.
13. DO obtain basic personal details from the witness.
14. DO make an investigation of the witness before interviewing, if possible.
15. DO find out where the witness may be reached, before he leaves.
16. DO impress the witness with the importance of what he has to tell you.
17. DO ascertain the sources of the witness's testimony.
18. DO attempt to determine the truthfulness of the witness's testimony.
19. DO let the witness tell his story in his own words.
20. DO make an estimate of the consistency of the witness's story.
21. DO get the witness's story before he can consult others.
22. DO attempt to ascertain the basis of the witness's recollection of important details.
23. DO question continuously--most people talk.
24. DO interview witnesses when they are "hot."
25. DO observe the behavior of the witness, his reaction to questions, his hesitancy and other qualities which characterize his responses.
26. DO note all contradictions.
27. DO obtain documentary evidence; when possible, the originals.
28. DO change interviewers, if you find that you are "stymied" with a particular witness.
29. DO remember that there are no hard and fast rules.
30. DO keep all promises made to a witness.
31. DO look the witness straight in the eye.

VI. INTERVIEWING DON'TS

1. DON'T be rude, officious or impolite. There is <u>matter</u> in manner.
2. DON'T antagonize the witness.
3. DON'T deny or dismiss reasonable requests of the witness once he has indicated that he is cooperating.
4. DON'T interview more than one witness at a time.
5. DON'T lose control over the conduct of the interview.
6. DON'T "wisecrack" during an interview.
7. DON'T cross-examine or "grill" the witness.
8. DON'T let the witness know the purpose of the interview.
9. DON'T let suspicion fall on a witness whom you think is suspect, during an interview.
10. DON'T allow the interview to be interrupted, if you can possibly avoid it.
11. DON'T use only the question and answer type of interview.
12. DON'T lose track of, or dismiss, the witness until you have obtained from him all the information that he has.
13. DON'T ask more than one question at a time.
14. DON'T persist in following an unsuccessful approach.
15. DON'T place much credence in hearsay.
16. DON'T tell the witness what the "story" is; let <u>him</u> do the talking.
17. DON'T necessarily disbelieve an entire statement just because part of it is untrue or inaccurate.
18. DON'T ignore valid documentary evidence in favor of oral testimony.
19. DON'T assume that the witness is familiar with maps or military terminology.
20. DON'T fail to evaluate information accurately.
21. DON'T fail to obtain corroboration of testimony, if possible.
22. DON'T let the witness know how much you know.
23. DON'T lose your temper.
24. DON'T use profane language.
25. DON'T ignore your senses or common sense.
26. DON'T overlook any leads given by the witness.
27. DON'T overlook any slips made by the witness.
28. DON'T argue with the witness.
29. DON'T indulge in personalities.
30. DON'T allow the information that you get to go stale.
31. DON'T allow your prejudices against the witness, or otherwise influence your evaluation of the witness's testimony.
32. DON'T forget to note the witness's behavior and movements, i.e. any hesitation in answering questions; uneasiness; inability to maintain eye contact.
33. DON'T forget that there are no hard and fast rules to interviewing.
34. DON'T lie to the witness or make threats.
35. DON'T forget to indicate the witness's ability in your opinion to recount the incident if necessary in front of a judge and jury.

VII. GETTING STARTED

1. Call the interviewee and introduce yourself, and explain the purpose for your call.

2. Be prepared to fully identify yourself and have a business card available.

3. Dress appropriately.

4. Make certain your batteries are charged and keep spares handy.

5. The first thing to do upon meeting the interviewee is to put him or her at ease. Don't make a big thing of your recording equipment; treat it as a natural part of the procedure. Answer any questions asked but don't volunteer unnecessary detail about what will or might be done with the recording. If pressed, you can truthfully minimize the likelihood of its use in court but make no guarantees.

6. Explain what you are going to do is to ask a few questions beforehand and then you will turn the machine on and go over the same facts.

7. Pre-interview the witness. Ask the questions you intend to ask for the record. This tends to relax the witness and also prepares you for areas of the story that you may want to go into more deeply. Before recording the statement ask the interviewee to have a pencil handy. Invite him/her to make a diagram of the accident as a guide of his/her description. This will help prevent the interviewee from contradiction.

8. It will be a good idea to tell the interviewee that some repetition will be necessary for purpose of identification and clarification.

9. Place the recording device <u>close to the interviewee</u>. He/she most likely will be the soft spoken one. You can always purposely speak louder.

10. Should an interruption occur by the other party or yourself, you should keep the recorder playing and comment to explain the interruption and that the recording will be continued in a few minutes.

12. If the recorder is turned off, you must ask your subject if he/she would like to discuss anything that was mentioned while the tape recorder was off. A few reasons for turning the machine off would be for the interviewee to answer the phone, door, clear up a complicated matter.

WHILE RECORDING

1. Begin the recording by following the opening statement in the statement guide. Be sure to include the question -- "Do I have your permission to record this interview?" You must also establish that the witness understands the conversation is being recorded and that you have his permission to do so.

2. At the beginning of the statement, you should identify people, places, time and what is being done.

3. You should also establish the fact that they are giving you the statement voluntarily, without the promise of any reward and under no circumstances which would constitute a threat or duress of any kind. You need to establish the subject's educational level and their ability to read, write and understand the English language. You also need to understand and establish your subject's control of their facilities by asking if they are under the influence of any drug, alcohol or medication of any kind at the time of the taping. If they are under a doctor's care and taking some type of drug, you may want to establish what that drug is and at what time it was last taken by your subject. If, at any point and time during this statement, while your subject is providing you with specific information about circumstances which are important to your case, and you have any suspicion that the subject is taking some sort of medication, uses drugs or is a drinker, you might want to again ask him or her if at the time they observed, heard or were involved in these circumstances were they under the influence of any drugs, alcohol or medication.

4. If you are taking statements from more than one person at the same location, separate them. Do not allow one to hear the other person's statement.

5. Use good statement taking techniques during the body of the recording. Control the conversation with the aid of your statement outline. Keep the information factual and use open-end questions beginning with <u>who</u>, <u>what</u>, <u>when</u>, <u>where</u>, <u>how</u>, etc.

6. It is also important that you take notes during this recorded statement. You should have also already taken notes during any statement made prior to the actual recorded statement. Both sets of notes should be available to you in order to formulate questions which will allow you to bring certain points out during the subject's statement.

7. End the recording, as suggested in the statement guide, by asking if there is anything you haven't covered, any pertinent facts, which are felt to be important. If so, let them come out freely. Then ask if he has understood all your questions and if his answers are true and correct to the best of his knowledge. Make sure the interviewee repeats his approval of having his statement recorded. A final "thank you" ends the recording.

AFTER RECORDING

1. After the recording and before you leave, run a spot-check on the record to make sure the machine was working.

2. As soon as possible, while the interview is still fresh, <u>summarize the important facts</u> and <u>your impression of the witness</u>. Indicate how the information developed in the statement may affect the client's decision to "contest" or "settle" the claim and the reasons for your conclusions. This information should be reported on in your report and comprise a vital part of the report conclusion.

3. In most cases your report will substitute for transcriptions of the recording so don't be afraid to elaborate in detail. Keep in mind that only at the request of the client will the record be transcribed.

4.   Your report and the electronic file (.wav or mp3) will then become a "material" part of the file. The statement file will be copied onto a CD and marked into evidence. Make certain that between the time you take the recording until you can download the file, the recorder is kept in a safe place.

5.   Remember you are not a licensed adjustor and should not be attempting to negotiate the settlement of a claim during your statement.

Please keep in mind that none of the following statement outlines in the manual are considered to be complete and comprehensive. Each case will warrant unique questions that apply to that case alone. They are merely outlines to reference and stimulate your own question-making process.

VIII. RECORDING TOOLS

It is always advised to take a statement in person so you can see the subject, study their body language and generally be more effective. However there will be cases where a statement may have to be taken over the phone. There are countless devices for taking statements over the phone from a landline. Most of these devices plug into the hand receiver and then have a separate mini jack that plugs into the recorder. When it comes to taking statement on your mobile phone, you will require an APP that allows you to download a program that will record both sides of the conversation. Your phone however may not be the best device and may have limitations of long statements so it's best to use a device that is specifically designed for this type of function. But some phones may not be  compatible with such voice recording applications. In these cases, you will again need to rely on some hardware. Sony makes a microphone that plugs into your digital recorder on one end and an ear piece on the other. The ear piece's primary purpose is to capture the phone conversation you hear as you place your cellular phone over the ear with the microphone ear piece. The device was release in 2012 and is called the Sony ECM-TL3 Earphone Style Mini Electret Condenser Microphone. I purchase my microphone ear piece on line through the Sony store for $19.99. Of course, in Florida you still need to notify the participants before recording any phone conversations. Even if the interview is not a formal statement, you can still tell the other party that the call is being recorded eliminating the challenges of having to write down all the information. It also prevents you from forgetting relevant information.

When choosing a digital recorder, make sure it allows you to download the file directly into your computer to transfer and save the file. Many recorders come with a separate USB wire and I have also found them with very nifty slide out USB connectors. These recorders can be found at large discount stores like WAL-MART or K-MART from around

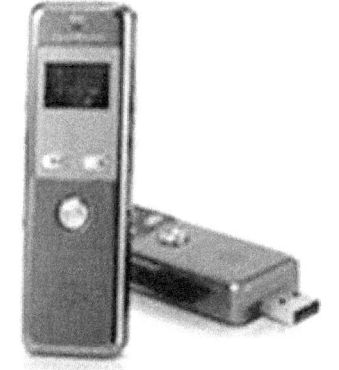

$25.00-$35.00. I am not a big believer in buying expensive equipment when there are so many devices that are reasonably priced and dependable. For many years now I have used the RCA VR5220-A Digital Recorder which takes two AAA batteries and has never let me down. Newer Digital Recorders will record files in MP3 which are smaller and easier to email. The newer recorders have climbed in pricing to over $50.00, but are well worth the extra money. The main key is that it has the capability to upload the statement to your computer. Some of the cheaper bands don't have USB upload which are of no value to the investigator so be careful.

After the recorded statement is over, you'll find yourself listening to the recording on your drive home or back to the office. This is the perfect time to recognize that you may have forgotten to ask a particular question. It's also the perfect time to call the subject back up and advise that you just realized you forgot to task them something. So get out your recorder and Sony earpiece and call them back to supplement the statement. Just start another recording and mention that this follow-up statement will supplement the previous statement taken.

IV. MAKING A CD COPY FOR CLIENT AND EVIDENCE

Once you're in the office, the statement will need to be downloaded to your computer. This is best done by following the instructions on your recorder. In most cases just by connecting your recorded to the computer, the software on the device will facilitate a download.

Set up a separate file on your computer marked "Statements" and make sure you drag and drop all recorded statements into this folder. The file names of the recorders will need to be changed during the transfer process so they are saved by witness/subject name.

Once the files as stored on your computer, you'll want to make two copies one for the client and one for the evidence room. DO NOT leave all your statement files on your computer without backing them up individually and numbering them individually (all evidence should be logged and numbered).

NERO

Is one of the more popular and mainstream software for copying data. Many of the basic versions are free to download. Once the software is downloaded onto your computer simply chose make a data disc and follow the prompts to browse for the file, in this case a statement or several statements and burn to disc. If you took multiple statements for one case, then there is no reason not to burn all of them on one disk (as long as they fit). Once a client's disk is made, simply duplicate the process and copy another disk to mark as evidence and store in an area away from your computer, typically a secure evidence room.

CHAPTER 2 -WORKERS' COMPENSATION STATEMENT OUTLINE

In preparation of recorded statement:

Before turning on recorder socialize briefly with the subject. Advise subject that they will need their driver's license number, previous addresses, names and addresses of hospitals, doctors and therapists. Also, subject should be prepared to identify prescription drugs and frequency of use, prior employers' names and addresses and information related to any previous insurance claims. Request that the subject gather the information before you turn on the recorder. Give the subject a general overview of what to expect during the interview.

Before turning on the recorder determine if the subject is on any medication. Make sure that this medication will not affect the subject's ability to give an accurate statement.

Introduction to Statement: **Turn on Recorder**

Today's date is _____. My name is (your name) and I am employed with Claims Resource Incorporated and represent (name of insurance company). I am at (the location where you are taking the statement from). I am interviewing (name of subject) who was involved in a workers' compensation accident. (Name of claimant), are you aware that I am recording this conversation: (Response). Do I have your permission to do so? (Response).

1. Personal History

    a. What is your full name and please spell your last name?
        1. Do you have any alias or nicknames?
        2. What is your maiden name?
        3. Have you ever had your name changed?
    b. What is your current address and how long have you been living at this location?
    c. Do you own or rent? Who is responsible for the care and upkeep of your home/lawn?
    d. What is your home phone number and an emergency phone number where you can be reached?
    e. What is your previous address? Did you rent or own?
    f. What is your date and place of birth?
    g. What is your social security number and driver's license number?
    h. Do you wear glasses/contacts?
    i. Do you smoke?
    j. What is the last grade you completed (high school, technical, trade school, or college?)
    k. Are you married? If so, what is your spouse's name?
    l. Do you have any dependents? (If yes name(s) and age(s). (Do they live at home?)
    m. What is the name and address of your closest living relative?
    n. Have you ever been convicted of a crime? (If yes, date(s), location,, charges, involved in a work release program).

2. Physical Description

    a. Provide me with a physical description of yourself: Race/color, sex, age, height, weight, hair length and color, facial hair, eye color, and any other identifying characteristics.

3. Current Employment/Insured

   a. What is the name and address of your current employer/insured?
   b. How long have you been employed with your current employer?
   c. What is your job title?
   d. What are your daily duties and responsibilities? (important)
   e. Are you a direct employee or independent contractor?
   f. Was an employment application required at time of hire?
   g. What is the name of your immediate supervisor?
   h. Wages
      1. What is your rate of pay?
      2. How many hours per week do you work?
      3. How many days per week to you work?
      4. Is overtime, room, board, meals, medical insurance or other benefits provided?

4. Other Sources of Income

   a. Were you employed at a second job while working for the insured? If so are you still employed at that job? (If yes, provide details, refer to section 3h-Wages).
   b. Is your spouse employed? (if yes, employer, wages and length of employment).
   c. Are you receiving social security benefits, unemployment, welfare, child support, insurance benefits or any other benefits? (If yes, determine value of benefits and how long they have been receiving).
   d. Do you have any other sources of income? (rental property, stocks, bonds, etc.)

5. Employment History

   a. Who have you worked for during the past five years?
      1. Location of employer
      2. Title and job duties
      3. Length of time at each job
   b. Did you serve time in the military?
      1. Military branch
      2. Date of discharge
      3. Any specialized training?
      4. Any injuries while in the military (If yes, where are the medical records kept?)

6. Off Hour Activities (Pre-Accident)

   a. Do you have any hobbies or are you involved in any sports or other recreational activities?
   b. How do you spend your free time? Organizations?
   c. What off hour activities were you involved in the two days leading up to the date of the accident?

(Determine if this person could have injured himself any other way).

7. ACCIDENT (See supplement for other types of questions)

   a. What is the date, time and place of the accident? (Be specific on the location).
   b. What time did you start work on the day of the accident?
   c. What activities were you involved in at work from the time you arrived until the time of the accident?
   d. Were you performing your usual job duties at the time of the accident?
   e. In your own words tell me exactly what happened.
      (Let the subject speak freely and do not interrupt).
      Take notes and ask follow-up questions later. Make sure you understand exactly how the accident occurred before proceeding. Most important part of the statement).
   f. Exactly what were you doing when the symptoms first appeared?
   g. Did you have anything in your hands at the time of the onset of the pain?
   h. What caused the accident to occur? (Slip, fall, lifting object or blow. If slip or fall, describe exactly how you landed and on what body part).
   g. Describe the pain you felt.
      1. When did you first feel the pain?
      2. What kind of pain did you feel? (Burning, dull, sharp, severe, radiating)
      3. Describe exact location of pain.
      4. Did you feel a snap, click or tearing of any part of the body? Where exactly?
      5. Was there arm or leg pain? Immediate or delayed?
      6. Did you feel a tingling present?
      7. If back injury, was there an inability to straighten up?
      8. Have you ever had similar pain or feeling? If so, when? How did it start, describe the pain or feeling and was there an medical treatment? By whom? Had it completely subsided? What caused it to reoccur? When was the last episode? Have you had continuous symptoms since then? How do they compare with the present symptoms?
      9. Had you taken any alcohol or chemical substance, prescription or otherwise into your body within 24 hours of the accident?
      10. Other than those injuries described are there any others?

8. Safety Equipment

   a. Were you using any safety devices? If yes, explain.
      1. Is the use of safety devices mandatory?
      2. Is the use of this equipment enforced?
      3. If not using, why not?

9. Witnesses

   a. Who did you first report the accident to:
      1. Name and title

  2. Date and time

 b. Was anyone working with you at the time of the accident? If yes, their title.
  1. If so, what were they doing?
  2. Were they involved in the accident or contribute to the accident in any way?

 c. Were there any other witnesses to the accident?
  1. List the names of any witnesses along with any other information that would assist us in locating these people.
  2. What was the witness doing at the time of the accident?
  3. What was the witness' reason for being in the area?

 d. Did any witness or anyone else contribute to the cause of the accident?

10. Injuries

 a. What did you do following the accident? Continue to work? Hospital?
 b. When did you first receive medical treatment? (If lapse in treatment, determine why).
 c. Who authorized medical treatment?
  1. Was a specific doctor and/or hospital recommended?
  2. What was said?
  3. Was the doctor/hospital a company approved facility?
 d. What are the name(s) of the <u>initial</u> examining and/or treating physicians?
  1. What type of treatment did you receive and what was the doctor's diagnosis? (Determine if x-rays were taken or any lab tests; when, where and outcome)
  2. Did you receive any medication or were you given a prescription for medication?
 e. What other doctor(s)/therapist(s) have you treated with since the time of the accident and their address.
  1. When and what treatment have you received?
  2. What was the diagnosis?
  3. Has the doctor given you any restrictions?
  4. What is your treatment program from this point forward?
  5. When is your next scheduled appointment?

11. Medication (current)

 a. Are you currently on any medication?
 b. What are you taking?
 c. What is it for? Is it working?
 d. How often do you take the medication?

12. Post-Accident Activities
 a. What have your activities been since the day of the accident?
 b. What have you not been able to do since the time of the accident?

c. When do you expect to return to work?
   d. If you are able to work in the same position, is there some other job you are capable of working?
   e. If you cannot return to this employer is there any other work you can or would like to do? Do you know where you can get that type of employment?

13. Third Party/Subrogation

   a. Was anyone else responsible for your injury? If so, why?
   b. Was accident caused by equipment failure? If yes, continue.
      1. Type of equipment, name of manufacturer, age of equipment.
      2. Any prior problems with equipment? Describe. If so, why did you continue to use it?
      3. Who is responsible for maintaining equipment?
      4. Was the equipment properly maintained?
      5. Is the maintenance service schedule available for review?
      6. Was operator (claimant or other) properly trained in the use of equipment?
      7. Were instructions being followed?
   c. If accident was caused by a third party (auto, contractor, etc.) explain.
      1. What is the name of the person or company and type of vehicle, if relevant, involved in the accident?
      2. Why were they in the area?
      3. How were they involved?
      4. Do you know the name of their insurance company. Are you contemplating a lawsuit against them?

14. Past Medical History

   a. Were you given a pre-employment physical?
   b. Do you have any pre-existing disabilities, diseases or impairments? If yes, was your employer aware of them?
      1. Who did you tell?
      2. When did you notify this person and under what circumstances?
      3. Did you list this disability/disease/ impairment on your employment application?
   c. What is the name and address of your current family physician?
   d. Have you ever had a prior injury to this body part(s) or any other body part?
   e. Have you had any prior injuries to any body part(s) that may have contributed to this accident?
   f. Have you ever had any prior injuries, diseases or surgeries? If yes, explain.
      1. Date
      2. Describe injury in detail and how it occurred.
      3. What treatment did you receive and by whom (Addresses)

15. Prior Insurance Claims

   a. Have you ever had a workers' compensation claim before? If so, provide details.

       b.   Have you ever had any other type of claim(s) against an insurance company? Such as auto, slip and fall, etc. (If already covered no need to go into detail)

16. Disability

       a.   What date did your current disability start and end?
       b.   Were you paid wages for the day of injury or any other part of your disability?

Statement Closing

Do you understand that if you work or receive income from any other source while receiving workers' compensation benefits you must immediately report the fact of the employment or monies received to the carrier or insurance company. (Response)

ASK: Is there anything else you would like to add or clarify in this statement before I conclude the recording? (If the response is no, proceed with the closing. If the response is yes, let the subject explain and ask follow-up questions if necessary. Once you are through, repeat this statement again before proceeding).

(Subject's Name), was everything you told me true and correct to the best of your knowledge and belief? (Subject's Name), were you aware that I was recording our conversation? Did I have your permission to do so? Would you please state your name for the final time? My name is (your name). Thank you for voluntarily giving this statement.

Upon request of client obtain appropriate releases and always attempt to photograph the subject.

AUTHORIZATION FOR MEDICAL AND WAGE INFORMATION

AUTHORIZATION FOR MEDICAL INFORMATION

To Whom It May Concern:

I hereby request and authorize you to disclose, whenever requested to do so by _____, its representative, any and all information you may have concerning _____ with respect to any illness or injury, medical history, consultation, prescription or treatment, including x-ray plates and copies of all hospital records.

A photo static copy of this authorization shall be considered as effective and valid as the original.

THIS IS NOT A RELEASE OF ANY CLAIM I MAY HAVE

Witness _____   Signed _____

Date _____

AUTHORIZATION FOR WAGE INFORMATION

To Whom It May Concern:

I hereby request and authorize you to disclose, whenever requested to do so by _____, representative, any and all information you may have concerning _____ with respect to any wage or benefits paid.

A photo static copy of this authorization shall be considered as effective and valid as the original.

THIS IS NOT A RELEASE OF ANY CLAIM I MAY HAVE

Witness _____   Signed _____

Date _____

AUTHORIZATION AND REQUEST FOR UNEMPLOYMENT COMPENSATION INFORMATION

DATE _____

IDENTIFICATION OF PARTIES	
NAME OF EMPLOYEE	SOCIAL SECURITY NO.
ADDRESS OF EMPLOYEE	DATE OF W.C. INJURY
EMPLOYER'S NAME	CARRIER'S FILE NO.
EMPLOYER'S ADDRESS	

EMPLOYEE'S AUTHORIZATION FOR RELEASE OF UNEMPLOYMENT COMPENSATION INFORMATION

NOTE: Section 440.15(10) Florida Statutes requires you to furnish this authorization for release upon demand by either the employer or carrier. Compensation payments will stop until you authorize the release of this information.

The Florida Workers' Compensation Act provides that my Workers' Compensation benefits shall be reduced by the amount of unemployment compensation received to allow determination of the proper amount of workers' compensation. I hereby authorize release of any unemployment compensation information relative to my account.

This authorization is valid for a period of 12 months from the date signed.

Employee _____   Date _____

RETURN TO	
Name	Address
Signature of Requesting Party	Title of Official

AUTHORIZATION AND REQUEST
FOR SOCIAL SECURITY INFORMATION

DATE _____

IDENTIFICATION OF PARTIES

NAME OF EMPLOYEE	SOCIAL SECURITY NO.
ADDRESS OF EMPLOYEE	DATE OF W.C. INJURY
EMPLOYER'S NAME	CARRIER'S FILE NO.
EMPLOYER'S ADDRESS	

EMPLOYEE'S AUTHORIZATION FOR RELEASE

TO: SOCIAL SECURITY ADMINISTRATION

The Florida Workers' Compensation Act provide that my worker's compensation benefits and my social security disability benefits combined may not exceed 80% of my average weekly wage. To allow determination of the proper amount of worker's compensation payments, I hereby authorize release of the information requested below.

Employee _____   Date _____

SOCIAL SECURITY INFORMATION

1. Has employee filed for social security disability benefits?
   (If "no", no other items need be answered) Yes / No

2. Have disability benefits to employee under 42 USC S423 and S402 been determined?
   (If "no", check item 3 if applicable and return one copy to requester) Yes / No

3. The information requested under item 4, Section III of this form will be furnished as soon as determination of benefits has been completed.

4. Periodic payments to worker (do not include payments to dependent)

Date Payments Began or Will Begin	Payment schedule - (Monthly, Weekly, etc.)	Initial Amount of Periodic Payment to Worker

ADDITIONAL INFORMATION REQUESTED

5. Periodic payments to Dependents

Date Payment Began or Will Begin	Payment Schedule - (Monthly, Weekly, etc.)	Initial Amount of Periodic Payment to Worker

6. Average Current Earnings (Monthly) _____
   Based on AMW _____   "High 5" _____   "High 1" _____

7. Have FICA wages been reported for worker for last two years? Yes / No

By Whom	Amount	Period Reported

RETURN TO

Name	Address

WORKERS' COMPENSATION BENEFITS

By signing this form, I acknowledge the following:

1. I am not eligible to receive temporary total disability payments if gainfully employed.

2. If I am receiving any type of disability compensation, I <u>must</u> notify my carrier of any and all sources of income, social security, cash or unemployment compensation I am receiving.

3. Failure to report any source of income while collecting disability benefits could result in possible criminal prosecution.

_____   _____
EMPLOYEE SIGNATURE   DATE

_____   _____
WITNESS   DATE

WORKERS COMPENSATION
SUPPLEMENTAL ACCIDENT QUESTIONS

This section contains some investigative questions for specific injuries mentioned below. These questions should be in conjunction with your regular workers' compensation fact statement. Once again, these questions are not considered to be complete and comprehensive. The questions should be used in conjunction with your own questions, those of the clients and general follow up questions which may arise from the discussion. Remember to listen carefully to all answers as follow up questions not covered in this outline are sure to be required in any statement.

1. Back Injury
2. Head Injury
3. Heart Attack
4. Heat Stroke
5. Assaults
6. Eye Injury
7. Dependent Claims
8. Dermatitis
9. Going & Coming Claims
10. Carpel Tunnel Syndrome
11. Knee Injury
12. Long shore and Harbor Workers Claims
13. Witness Statements

BACK INJURY INTERVIEW

ACCIDENT (SUPPLEMENTAL QUESTIONS)

a. Exactly what was claimant doing when symptoms first appeared?
b. Anything in hands at onset of pain?
c. Exact mechanism of incident--slip, fall, lift or blow? If fall, describe exactly how landed and on what part of body.
d. Description of pain.
   1. What was first noticed?
   2. What kind of pain - sharp, dull, severe, burning?
   3. Describe exact site of pain.
      Any other parts of body involved? Rule out involvement of other parts of the body and pinpoint trauma.
   4. Was there a snap, click or tearing in back? Pinpoint area of back---at waist, between shoulders, etc.
   5. Was there leg pain or arm pain? Immediate or delayed? Trace exact pain down leg or arm.
   6. Was parathesia (tingling) present?
   7. Was there inability to straighten up? Temporary paralysis of legs?
   8. Have you ever had similar pain or feeling? If so, when (exact date), how did it start, describe the pain or feeling and was there any medical attention? By whom? Had it completely subsided? What caused it to reoccur? When was last episode? Continuous symptoms since then? How do they compare with the present symptoms?
   9. Had you taken any alcohol or chemical substance, prescription or otherwise into your body within 24 hours prior to the injury/
e. Description of activities after accident.
   1. Immediately--did he quit at once or finish the day or shift?
   2. Activities since day of incident?
   3. Any lost time--give dates.
   4. Has he/she been paid for time lost? What was first day not paid?
   5. If losing time, when can he/she return to work?

HEAD INJURY INTERVIEW

ACCIDENT

a. If injury caused by fall
    10. From where did he/she fall?
    2. What distance did he/she fall?
    3. Did he/she strike anything on the way down?
    4. What did he/she land on?
    5. Specifically, what part of the body struck first?

b. If injury caused by falling object
    1. From where did it fall?
    2. What distance did it fall?
    3. How heavy was the object?
    4. Describe the object as to shape and bulk.
    5. Specifically, what part of the head did it strike?
    6. Did it strike any other part of the body or cause injury to any other part of the body?
    7. Did the claimant fall to the ground?

c. Was he/she unconscious? If so, for how long?
d. Did he/she raise himself from the fall without assistance? If not, who assisted?
e. Did he/she bleed from the mouth, nose or ear?
f. Were there marks on his/her face or head? Scratches, bruises, cuts? Describe.
g. Did he/she speak coherently following the accidently?
h. Was he/she able to walk unassisted?
i. Was disability immediate? If not, when did it occur?
j. Last day worked? Last day paid? When can he/she return to work? Has he/she discussed with employer?
k. Had he/she taken any alcohol or chemical substance, prescription or otherwise, into his/her body within 24 hours of accident?

HEART ATTACK INTERVIEW

IN ORDER FOR A HEART ATTACK CLAIM TO BE COMPENSABLE UNDER FLORIDA WORKERS' COMPENSATION LAW, THE EMPLOYEE MUST HAVE BEEN DOING SOMETHING UNUSUAL TO HIS REGULAR DUTIES UNDER VERY UNUSUAL CIRCUMSTANCES

ACCIDENT

a. Describe the specific detailed symptoms on the date of the alleged injury. Cover exactly what the person was doing when the symptoms were first noted and activities immediately after the symptoms were noted.

b. Give special attention to whether he/she can describe any shortness of breath, pain in the chest, tiredness, headaches, dizziness, radiating pain from the chest, arms, etc. If these came on gradually, cover exactly when they were first noticed and under what circumstances. If he/she had them before, cover the past history in detail, paying special attention to time between one attack and another.

c. Cover the activities he/she performed on the day the attack came on at work, in detail, paying particular attention to whether there were any unusual activities. If any lifting or straining involved, cover in detail.

d. Cover whether he/she has been forced because of the job to work any unusually long hours or under unusual stress or strain of any type.

e. If he/she feels the attack is due to his/her work, why?

f. Cover whether there were any stresses or strains in his/her home life, such as family trouble, financial trouble, recent deaths, trouble with children, etc.

g. If there was any specific injury connected with the onset of the attack, describe exactly what the claimant was doing when it occurred?
   1. Was the injury caused by fall or was he/she struck by something?
   2. From what distance did he/she fall and what did he/she strike?
   3. Specifically cover what apart of his/her body was struck, trying to rule out any injury in the chest area.

h. Describe in detail how he/she has felt from the time the symptoms were first noted until the present time. Was there any time when the symptoms went away and he/she was free from any pain, etc. If so, cover in detail.

HEAT STROKE INTERVIEW

ACCIDENT

a. How did the claimant feel when he/she came to work the morning of the incident? Describe in detail any problems.
b. Exact work he/she had performed prior to becoming ill. Length of time worked prior to becoming ill.
c. What symptoms did he/she first notice? Did he/she collapse? The time element between the onset of the symptoms and the collapse, if any
d. Did he/she tell anyone of not feeling well prior to his collapse. Who and when? Cover his/her exact complaints.
   1. Any aches, dizziness, or problems seeing?
   2. Temperature, if any?
   3. Condition of his/her skin--cold or heated and sweaty, etc.?
   4. Did he/she feel faint or collapse?
   5. Rapid pulse?
   6. Nausea?
e. Was he/she working outside or inside?
   1. If outside, was he/she in a ditch or trench, or any other diggings? Describe in detail.
f. Was he/she allowed breaks to go inside to cool off, get drink of water, etc.? If so, how long in between and how long were the breaks?
g. Any accidental injury or trauma prior to the heat stroke symptoms?
h. What doctor did he/she see and when?
i. Cover past medical history in detail, especially any prior episodes of fainting or heat stroke.
j Get date of last physical exam and name of doctor.
k. Name and address of family physician and date of last examination. For what reason? Results?
l. Cover condition and complaints at time of this statement.
m. Names, addresses, employers or witnesses.
n. How was he/she transported to medical treatment?

IT IS SUGGESTED THAT IMMEDIATE AUTHORIZATION BE OBTAINED FROM THE ADJUSTER TO CONTACT THE EMPLOYER AND THE FOLLOWING STATEMENT BE TAKEN FROM THEM.

Insured

Contact immediate supervisor and find out how and when they first received notice of the claim.
1. Exact duties of the claimant.
2. Physical conditions of work area, including type of ventilation, if any.
3. Have any other employees complained of similar problems? Where, when and who?
4. Does the claimant have any restrictions on the type of work he/she can perform?

ASSAULT INTERVIEW

There are several general rules to consider. Usually the assault cases are compensable if the reason for the quarrel originates from the work or if the employment increases the risk of the assault. One of the strongest considerations, however, is who actually struck the first blow as the aggressor.

They are usually not compensable if the quarrel arises strictly because of personal reasons or if the claimant was the aggressor.

The statement should be focused on determining the above.

ACCIDENT

a. Names and addresses and employers of involved persons.
b. Length of time each worked for the employer.
c. Exact duties of each, cover how often and under what circumstances they come in contact with each other during the day.
d. Cover their past relationship and any history of conflict must be covered in detail.
e. Did either party have weapons?
f. When did present trouble start? Cause?
g. How long did it last? Hours, days, etc.?
h. Any "cooling-off period" between any arguments and the actual assault--cover in detail.
i. Who started the argument and for what reason?
j. Who delivered the first blow?
k. Had either party had any alcohol or chemical substance intake within 24 hours of altercation?

LONGSHORE AND HARBORWORKER INTERVIEW

ACCIDENT

a. Date, time and place of accident.
b. In own words, tell exactly what happened.
c. Exact location of accident
    1. Within state limits?
    2. How far from nearest shoreline?
    3. Was it on or adjacent to navigable waters?
    4. Was it on-board a vessel?
        (a) What type of vessel or platform was it?
        (b) Purpose of vessel?
        (c) Who owns the vessel?
        (d) Is it under charter? What kind?
        (e) Length of vessel?
        (f) Tonnage of vessel?
d. Exactly what was the claimant doing when symptoms first appeared?
e. Description of injury - cut, bruise, strain, etc.
    1. What was first noticed?
    2. What kind of pain-sharp, dull, severe, etc.
    3. Describe exact site of pain, exactly, including <u>all</u> parts of the body in pain. Be specific including every injury or parts involved.
f. Had you taken any alcohol or chemical substance, prescription or otherwise into your body within 24 hours prior to the injury?
g. Description of activities after accident.
    1. Immediately - did he quit at once or finish the day or shift?
    2. Activities since day of incident?
    3. Any lost time - give dates.
    4. Has he been paid for time lost? What was the first day not paid?
    5. If losing time, when can he return to work?

KNEE INJURY INTERVIEW

ACCIDENT

a. Date, time and place of accident.
b. In own words, tell exactly what happened.
c. Exactly what was claimant doing when symptoms first appeared?
d. Anything in hands at onset of pain?
e. What parts of the body specifically were involved? (Be sure to specify left, right, thigh, lower leg, etc.)
f. Description of symptoms
   1. What was first noticed?
   2. Describe pain - sharp, dull, severe, throbbing, etc.
   3. Are any other parts of the body in pain?
   4. Was there any snap, click, tearing, grinding, popping, etc.?
   5. Any swelling? When did it begin?
   6. Any movement of the kneecap?
   7. Exactly what area of the knee is painful? (front, back, side, above, below, etc.)
   8. Is knee "hot" to touch (fevered)?
   9. Have you had any similar pain or feeling before? If so, when and was there treatment? By whom? Had it completely subsided? What caused it to reoccur? When was last episode? Continuous symptoms since then? How do they compare with current symptoms?
g. Had you consumed any alcohol or chemical substance, prescription or otherwise within 24 hours of the accident?
h. Description of activities since accident.

DEPENDENCY CLAIM INTERVIEW

I. Name, permanent address, phone, age, date of birth, citizenship?

II. Where and when married to deceased - view and get copy of marriage certificate.

III. Any divorce proceeding or separation in present marital setup?

IV. Any prior marriages of claimant?
  A. Date and place?
  B. Children by that marriage? Age of children, married, address, adoption? View copies of birth certificates and describe. Obtain copies.
  C. Divorced - when and where (city and county).

V. Any prior marriages of deceased?
  A. Date and place (city and county)
  B. Children by that marriage, age of children, married, address, adoption? Copies of birth certificates?
  C. Divorced - when and where (city and county). Any alimony or support payments of any kind?

VI. Names, address, ages of any dependents who are dependents because of a disability, either mental or physical - describe.

VII. Names, addresses, ages of any dependents who are dependents because of a disability, either mental or physical - describe.

VIII. Common law marriages
  A. Where is the relationship alleged to have been entered into?
  B. All jurisdictions in which the couple lived together and dates they lived there.
  C. Why no ceremony performed. If one was performed later, give circumstances.
  D. Did couple hold themselves as husband and wife?
  E. Did others in the locality recognize them as husband and wife? Get names and addresses of neighbors so believing.
  F. Did they ever intend to have a genuine ceremonial wedding?
  G. When did they intend or agree to be husband and wife.

IX. Other dependents
  A. Exact relationship to deceased.
  B. Amount of payments and method of payments. Get breakdown of household expenses. Regularity of contributions. Any written record of cancelled checks?
  C. Who else contributes and how much to this person's support?
  D. What assets does dependent have? Bank account, real estate, personal property, stock and bonds, pension funds, social security.

X. How much is funeral bill? Has it been paid? Any outstanding medical bills?

XI. Anything claimant wishes to add? Standard close.

DERMATITIS CLAIM INTERVIEW

There are many kinds of dermatitis and they can be caused by almost any sort of allergy inside or outside of the employment. These facts are needed to provide the medical consultant with proper background for opinion.

In some cases, the employee will not be off work very long, but the medical expense can be great because it is often necessary for him to undergo a long program of desensitization therapy. Most of these claims are questionable and the attending physician does not always call in a dermatologist. If you will cover the following points in claims of this nature, we will have a reasonably complete investigation on which either the adjuster can make a decision or refer the facts to a specialist for an intelligent honest opinion.

1. The usual introductory paragraph will include the employee's name, age, wage information, marital status, education, occupation history and military information.

2. How long has the claimant worked for our insured?

3. Was he/she ever bothered with a similar condition prior to entering our insured's employment? If so, what type of work was he/she doing at the time and was the cause of the condition determined?

4. What substance does he/she usually come in contact with in his/her work? Include types of chemicals, greases or oils, soaps, types of dust, TRADE names, etc.

5. What type of work has he/she been doing about the time he/she first noticed this condition and approximately when was he/she first afflicted?

6. Does he/she know of any other employees at our insured's place of business who have been similarly afflicted?

7. Does the dermatitis get worse while he/she is at work or at home? Does it get worse while he/she is doing any particular kind of work or working with any particular kind of chemical? Does it seem to get better while he/she is away on vacation or over weekends and away from his/her work?

8. Has he/she ever been bothered with hay fever, asthma, any particular type of plant poisoning, migraine headaches, ringworm, athlete's foot, any other fungus infection of skin disease?

9. Describe the nature of his/her employment in detail, including any peculiarities or his/her particular type of work.

10. Describe his/her outside activities, covering particularly whether or not he/she keeps a garden or works with plants, develops his/her own pictures, or any other hobby which would bring him/her into contact with some sort of chemical which could cause such a condition.

11. What brand of cosmetics, lotions, soaps, and deodorants does the employee use?

12. Describe the nature of his/her previous work with other employers, the length of service in each and the names and addresses of his/her previous employers.

13. Describe the appearance of the dermatitis and its later development, particularly naming the exact portion of the body where he/she first broke out and naming the other portions of the body to which it has spread.

"GOING AND COMING" CLAIM INTERVIEW

The first criteria of any claim being held compensable is whether or not the claimant was about the employer's business and whether or not the employer derives benefit from the claimant being where he/she was. This is even stronger in "going and coming" claims.

In order for the claim to be compensable, the following criteria must be met:

1. The claimant has to have been about the employer's business or that had to have been the purpose of the trip.
2. He/she had to have been instructed to run an errand or do the business, either by someone in a supervisory capacity, or it must have been a routine in his/her general job description.
3. There could not have been any deviation in the direct route to or from the place of duty, unless specifically agreed upon by the employer, i.e., first going to lunch, then business, etc. If this is the case, there still should be a direct route established.
4. The employee is on call. Management called to work for a specific reason is covered. Salespeople entertaining clients are covered, etc.

Your task is to cover the following:

5. The reason for the trip.
6. The route and time taken.
7. Any deviation from the direct route and why.
8. The time, as exact as possible, taken for each activity.
9. Who established the necessity for the trip?
10. The benefit derived by the employer from the trip.
11. Any subrogation possibility.

IT IS, OF COURSE, THE RESPONSIBILITY OF THE INVESTIGATOR TO GATHER THE INFORMATION. ONLY THE ADJUSTER HANDLING THE CLAIM WILL BE ABLE TO MAKE THE FINAL DETERMINATION OF COMPENSABILITY.

The Incident

    A. Date, time and place of accident.
    B. In own words, tell exactly what happened.
    C. Was accident on company property?
    D. What was purpose of travel away from employer's premises?
        1. Was claimant running an errand?
            a. Describe the nature of the errand.
            b. Under whose instructions was he acting?
                (1) What is their capacity with employer?
                (2) Was the business personal or for the benefit of the employer?

- c. Track exact route and time to and from the errand.
- d. Was claimant in company or personal vehicle?
- e. Is this part of regular duties?
- f. If in personal car, are they reimbursed mileage/expenses or are they compensated in any way for this?

2. Was claimant on way to work or returning home from work, or at lunch?
   - a. What are regular working hours?
   - b. Was claimant "on call" that day or is he <u>ever</u>?
   - c. Did someone instruct him to come in early or leave late?
     - (1) Who did so?
     - (2) For what reason?

3. If accident happened during work hours:
   - a. What was reason for claimant being off premises?
   - b. Does employer provide place for employees to eat lunch or must he/she go off premises to eat or buy food?
   - c. Was any business taken care of at lunch?
   - d. Track exact route and time period to and from errands or business for entire time off premises.
   - e. Whose instructions were for claimant to leave premises?
   - f. Is this claimant's regular duties?
   - g. Were instructions carried out prior to accident?

4. If the claimant was on foot...
   - a. Purpose of business.
   - b. Mechanism of accident.
     - (1) Struck by vehicle
       - (a) Who owned?
       - (b) Driver?
       - (c) Who investigated accident?
     - (2) If tripped, slipped or fell
       - (a) What caused fall?
       - (b) Who maintains property? Who cleans floors?
       - (c) Was anyone else responsible?

E. Was claimant wearing seat belt?
F. What law enforcement agency investigated?
   1. Does claimant have copy of report?
   2. Who was charged with the accident?
G. Were there any passengers in the claimant's vehicle?
H. Had the claimant had any alcohol or chemical intake, prescription or otherwise within 24 hours of the accident?

CARPAL TUNNEL SYNDROME INTERVIEW

Carpal Tunnel Syndrome is caused by a thickening of the cartilage in the wrist. This is usually caused by one of the follow:

1. Natural aging process, particularly in women of menopausal age (non-compensable).
2. Repetitive trauma caused by repeated hand twisting of the wrist area, as in assembly line, etc. (compensable).
3. Sudden trauma to rigid wrists, such as falling on outstretched hands, bracing the body with the hands and wrist against a steering wheel, etc.

Usually carpal tunnel syndrome appears six (6) weeks or more following a sudden trauma. It is not unusual for someone who has broken an arm to develop this complaint.

This condition is first manifest by tingling and pain in the ring and little fingers, soon awakening the patient during the night and, in more advanced stages, pain and swelling and loss of feeling during waking hours, causing the patient to drop things. etc.

<u>The Incident</u>

    A. Was there any sudden trauma? Date, time, place?
        1. In own words, describe how the incident happened?
        2. How were hands/wrists/arms involved?
        3. If claimant fell, exactly how did he/she land?
        4. Did any object strike the claimant?
    B. If symptoms appeared over a period of time.
        1. When did the symptoms first appear?
        2. What made symptoms worse?
        3. What job were they performing at that time?
            a. Any machinery, tools or equipment involved?
            b. How? What do they do that is strenuous?
    C. Which hand/hands involved?
    D. Describe exact symptoms.
        1. Pain? What kind?
        2. Tingling? (parathesia)
        3. What part of hand involved? Which fingers?
        4. Is arm involved and if so, what area? What symptoms?
    E. Any inability to use hand?
    F. Any other part of the body involved/
    G. Any pain in neck, head, shoulder area?
        1. Describe pain.
        2. When did pain first appear?

       3.   Why are these other areas, if any, involved? Were they injured from this accident or is pain just radiating into these areas?
- H.   Have symptoms been continuous? Any previous paid on symptoms such as these?
- I.   Has he/she lost any time from work? Have they been paid for time off?
- J.   Any other routine activities been interrupted?

EYE INJURY INTERVIEW

The Incident

- K.   Date, time and place of accident.
- L.   In own words, tell exactly what happened.
- M.   Exact description of what was being done when alleged injury occurred.
- N.   When was first day off of work? Has he/she been paid for time off?
- O.   Did anything strike the eyeball? What?
- P.   Did anyone examine the eyeball? Who? When? What observations were made? Was a foreign body observed? If so, was it removed? Describe foreign body removed.
- Q.   If detached retina, develop the following:
    1. Exact time (day and hour) when visual loss was discovered. How was it discovered? What was claimant doing when the loss became evident? To whom did he/she report it and what did he/she tell that person?
    2. If the visual loss is attributed to a lift, jar, bump or blow, secure the details about the exact time of that event, the mechanism involved, and spell out the severity of it. Also, identify the symptoms, if any, observed at the time of the event up to the time of the first recognition of visual loss. If there was a symptom free period, give the exact dates. Cover outside activities prior to the work connected incident alleged to the time that visual loss was observed. What outside activities embraced lifting, bumps, blow or jars?
- R.   Was process complete before pain or irritation felt? What were first symptoms noticed? When? Describe.
- S.   Complete day's work?

WORKERS' COMPENSATION WITNESS STATEMENT QUESTIONS

1. Witness Statement - Eyewitness to Injury

2. Witness Statement - Unwitnessed Injury

3. Foreman's Supervisor's Statement - Eyewitness

4. Foreman's/Supervisor's Statement - Unwitnessed injury

WITNESS STATEMENT - EYEWITNESS TO INJURY

1. Name - spell out.
2. Complete address.
3. Name, address and phone number of someone who will always know your whereabouts.
4. Age and birth date.
5. By whom are you employed? Name, street address, city and state
6. What is your position with them? What department?
7. How long have you been employed by them?
8. Are you acquainted with (claimant)?
9. Will you describe his work for duties for me?
10. Do you recall (claimant) getting hurt? (Affirmative answer).
11. When did this happen? Date and time.
12. Where did this happen?
13. Where were you when this happened? (With claimant, nearby, etc.).
14. Did you see him/her get hurt?
15. Will you describe in your own words what you saw?
16. Injury-Complaint-Medical - use applicable questions.
    a. What did you observe (claimant) injuries to be? (Be specific. ON falls and head injuries cover unconsciousness and bleeding from ears, nose and mouth).
    b. What complaints did (claimant) make at that time? (On strains and sprains like back, arm, hernia, etc., pinpoint the areas of pain).
    c. What happened to him/her after this? (cover referral to plant clinic, M.D., nurse, hospital, etc.)
    d. Have you seen him/her since this occurred?
    e. What did you observe about his/her condition?
17. Third party or objected involved. Pursue on malfunctioning of machines, off premises, auto and construction accidents.
18. When did he/she first lose time from work?
19. Has he/she returned to work?
20. Do you know of any other witnesses to this incident? If no, ask.
21. What other employees work near or with (claimant)?
22. Do you know of any previous injuries to (claimant)? Details.
23. Do you know of him/her ever making these complaints before?
24. Do you know of him/her working for anyone else outside of your company? Details.
25. Standard concluding questions.

WITNESS STATEMENT - UNWITNESSED INJURY

1. Name - spell out.
2. Home address.
3. Name, address and phone number of someone who will always know your whereabouts.
4. Age and birth date.
5. By whom are you employed? Name, street address, city and state.
6. What is your position with them?
7. How long have you been employed by them? What department?
8. Are you acquainted with (claimant)?
9. Do you work with him/her?
10. Will you describe his/her duties for me?
11. Are you aware of (claimant) complaining about (name of injury or complaint)?
12. When did you first learn of this? (date, time and place).
13. How did you first learn of his complaints? (claimant in person, telephone, fellow worker, relative).
14. What were you told at that time by (informant above)?
15. Have you seen him since learning of his/her complaints?
16. Did you report this to anyone in the company? (Identify, date, time and place).
17. What did you observe about his/her condition?
18. Did you report this to anyone in the company? (Identify, date, time and place).
19. Third party or object involved. Pursue on malfunctioning of machines, off premises, auto and construction accidents.
20. Disability - use applicable questions.
    a. When did (claimant) first start losing time from work? (date).
    b. Is he/she still off OR has he/she returned to work? (date).
21. Do you know of anyone who is alleged to have witnessed the accident? (details).
22. Do you know of anyone else who know of his/her complaints?
23. What employees work with or near (claimant) who might have witnessed the incident?
24. Do you know of (claimant) ever making these complaints before? (details).
25. Do you know of any other previous injuries to him/her? (details).
26. Does he/she have any other employment to your knowledge? (details).
27. Standard concluding questions.

FOREMAN'S OR SUPERVISOR'S STATEMENT - EYEWITNESS INJURY

1. Name - spell out.
2. Complete address.
3. Age and birth date
4. Name, address and phone number of someone who will always know your whereabouts.
5. By whom are you employed?
6. What is your position with them? What department?
7. How long have you been employed by present employer?
8. As (title of person) are you acquainted with (claimant's name)?
9. Are you his/her immediate supervisor? (If not, determine who is).
10. Would you describe (claimant's name) work or duties for me?
11. Do you recall (claimant) getting hurt? (Affirmative answer).
12. When did this happen? (Date and time).
13. Where did this happen?
14. Where were you when this happened?
15. Did you see it happen?
16. Will you describe in your own words what you saw happen?
17. Was he/she working on his/her regular job when this happened?
18. Did you make a report of this to anyone in the company? (Get details).
19. Injuries-Complaints-Medical-use applicable questions.
    a. What did you observe (claimant) injuries to be? Be specific. On falls and head injuries cover unconsciousness and bleeding from ears, nose and mouth).
    b. What complaints did (claimant) make at the time? (On strain and sprain cases like back, hernia, arms, etc., pinpoint areas of complaints of pain).
    c. Did you send him/her to anyone for treatment (or examination)? (Cover when and identify M.D., hospital, clinic, nurse, etc.) OR
    d. Did he/she request any medical treatment? (If so, determine what foreman did per "c" above).
    e. Have you seen him/her since this occurred?
    f. What did you observe his condition to be?
20. Third party or object involved. Pursue on malfunctioning of machines, off premises, auto and construction accidents.
21. When did (claimant) first start losing time from work?
22. Is he/still off work? Has he/she returned to work? If so, when?
23. Do you know of any other witnesses to this incident?
24. What employees work with or near (claimant) who might have witnessed the incident?
25. Do you know of prior accidents to (claimant)? Get details.
26. Do you know of (claimant) working for anyone else outside of your company? If so, get details.
27. Standard concluding questions.

FOREMAN'S OR SUPERVISOR'S STATEMENT - UNWITNESSED INJURY

1. Name - spell out.
2. Complete address.
3. Age and birth date
4. Name, address and phone number of someone who will always know your whereabouts.
5. By whom are you employed?
6. What is your position with them? What department?
7. How long have you been employed by present employer?
8. As (title of person) are you acquainted with (claimant's name)?
9. Are you his/her immediate supervisor? (If not, determine who is).
10. Would you describe (claimant's name) work or duties for me?
11. Are you aware of (claimant) complaining about (name injury and complaint).
12. When did you first learn of his/her complaints? (From who, claimant, fellow workers, relative. How? In person? Telephone?)
13. What were you told by the informant?
14. Were any other complaints made? If so, get details.
15. Did you look into his/her complaints? What did you find?
16. Based on your investigation of his/her complaints, was he/she injured on his/her regular job?
17. Have you seen (claimant) since learning of his/her complaints?
18. If yes, what did you observe about his/her condition?
19. Did you make a report of (claimant) complaints to anyone in the company? (Identify, date and time).
20. Third party or object involved. Pursue on malfunctioning of machines, off premises, auto and construction accidents.
21. Medical treatment - use applicable questions.
    a. Did (claimant) state he/she was being treated? If yes, identify doctor and/or hospital.
        1. Was this your first knowledge of this treatment?
        2. Did you tell him/her to continue with treatment?
        3. Did you send him/her to anyone else? If yes, identify.
    b. Did (claimant) request any medical treatment? (If so, what did foreman do per "c" below?).
    c. Did you send (claimant) to anyone for treatment or examination? (Cover when and identify M.D., hospital, clinic, nurse, etc.).
22. When did (claimant) first start losing time from work?
23. Is he/she still off work? Has he/she returned to work? If so, when?
24. Do you know of anyone who is alleged to have witnessed accident? Get details.
25. What employees work with or near (claimant) who might have witnessed the incident?
26. Do you know of anyone else who knows of his/her complaints?
27. Do you know of (claimant) ever making these complaints before? Details.
28. Do you know of any previous injuries to (claimant). Details.
29. Do you know of (claimant) working for anyone else outside of your company? If so, get details.
30. Standard concluding questions.

CHAPTER 3 AUTOMOBILE LIABILITY

GENERAL FACT STATEMENT

In preparation of recorded statement:

Before turning on recorder socialize briefly with the subject. Advise the subject they will need their driver's license number, previous addresses, names and addresses of hospitals, doctors and therapists. The subject should be prepared to identify prescription drugs and frequency of use, prior employers' names and addresses and information related to any previous insurance claims. Request that the subject gather the information before you turn on the recorder. Give the subject a general overview of what to expect during the interview.

Before turning on the recorder determine if the subject is on any medication. Make sure that this medication will not effect the subject's ability to give an accurate statement.

Introduction to Statement: **Turn on Recorder**

Today's date is _____. My name is (your name) and I am employed with Claims Resource Incorporated and represent (name of insurance company). I am at (the location where you are taking the statement from). I am interviewing (name of subject) who was involved in a workers' compensation accident. (Name of claimant), are you aware that I am recording this conversation: (Response). Do I have your permission to do so? (Response).

1. Personal History

    a. What is your full name and please spell your last name?
        1. Do you have any alias or nicknames?
        2. What is your maiden name?
        3. Have you ever had your name changed?
    b. What is your current address and how long have you been living at this location?
    c. Do you own or rent? Who is responsible for the care and upkeep of your home/lawn?
    d. What is your home phone number and an emergency phone number where you can be reached?
    e. What is your previous address? Did you rent or own?
    f. What is your date and place of birth?
    g. What is your social security number and driver's license number?
    h. Do you wear glasses/contacts?
    i. Do you smoke?
    j. What is the last grade you completed (high school, technical, trade school, or college?)
    k. Are you married? If so, what is your spouse's name?
    l. Do you have any dependents? (If yes name(s) and age(s). (Do they live at home?)

m. What is the name and address of your closest living relative?
   n. Have you ever been convicted of a crime? (If yes, date(s), location,, charges, involved in a work release program).

2. Vehicle ID
   a. What is the year and make of the vehicle you were driving?
   b. Color?
   c. License number?
   d. Legal and registered? (also mat of other party)
   e. Was there any previous damage to your vehicle (especially if older vehicles)?

3. Scene
   a. Direction?
   b. Speed?
   c. Lane of travel?
   d. Distance when you first saw the other vehicle?
   e. The estimated speed?
   f. Direction lane?
   g. Color signal?
   h. Any skid marks left by either vehicle?
   i. Length of skids?
   j. Point of impact on the street and to the cars?
   k. Evasive action?
   l. Sudden stop - why?
   m. Were the police called?
   n. Who called them?
   o. Were there any witnesses, names, addresses, phone, statements?
   p. Were any citations issued?
   q. Arrests?
   r. Drug or alcohol involvement?
   s. Were there any visual obstructions?
   t. Any conversation after the accident with other driver?
   u. Exchange of names and addresses?
   v. Did anyone admit fault?
   w. Any corrective action taken by other vehicle?
   x. Who do you feel is at fault? Any why?

5. Passengers
   a. Number of occupants in your vehicle?
   b. Position in vehicle?
   c. Names, age address, phone.
   d. Describe them.

6. Injuries

    a.   Was anyone injured?
    b.   Describe injuries.
    c.   Describe how injuries occurred.
    d.   Did you see the accident coming?
    e.   Did you brace for impact? How?
    f.   Position of body and head at impact.
    g.   Movement of body and head at impact.
    h.   Did any body part strike interior of vehicle? Get specifics.
    i.   Describe the headrests in the vehicle.
    j.   Did any flying object in vehicle strike body?
    k.   Did you sustain any lacerations?
    l.   Bruises?
    m.   Were you bleeding?
    n.   Did you lose consciousness after impact? Why? How long?
    o.   Were any passengers injured? (if so, ask same series of injury questions).

7. Impact
    a.   Did your head hit the headrest?
    b.   What was the position of your head when it hit the headrest?
    c.   How far (forward, backward) did your head move at impact?
    d.   Speed of vehicle at impact?
    e.   Does vehicle have seat belts? Shoulder harness? Were they in use? Did the seat belt lock? Did it fail?
    f.   Did seat move forward at impact?
    g.   What was vehicle movement subsequent to impact? Distance traveled after impact.
    h.   Does vehicle have air bag? Did it deploy?
    i.   Does vehicle have impact bumper shocks?
    j.   On a scale of 1 to 10, how would you rank this impact if 1 is equivalent to one car rolling into another and 10 is a head-on crash on the freeway?
    k.   Did this impact resemble an experience you have had driving or otherwise? (For example, bumping into a parking curb, bumping into someone in a crowd, amusement park ride)

8. Priors
    a.   Any prior injuries from accident of any type? What? When?
    b.   Any prior chiro/acupuncture/PT treatment for maintenance?
    c.   Over what period of time? Frequency? Diagnosis?

9. Pain at Scene
    a.   When was onset of pain? Where was pain? Give comprehensive description.
    b.   Ambulance requested at scene? If no, why not?
    c.   Any seat belt bruises? Describe.
    d.   Did you drive vehicle from scene?
    e.   Did you continue to same destination?

10. Treatment
    a. Who are you seeing for this injury?
    b. Type of doctor? Type of treatment? Describe both in detail.
    c. When were you first seen?
    d. Who referred you and when? Have you ever seen this doctor before for any reason?
    e. Who administers the treatment and how long does it last?
    f. Do you use a sign-in sheet?
    g. Who is paying for TX? Do you know how much the bill is?
    h. Who is your regular family doctor? (GYN, Pediatrician)
    i. Are you work disabled? Period of time? Describe restrictions.
    j. Is TX helping you to return to pre-accident status?
    k. Any permanency expected?
    l. If late treatment, explain why.
    m. Have injuries changed lifestyle? Sports, aerobics, church, amusement, shopping?
    n. Is there anything you can't do today that you were able to do before this accident?

11. Claim Information
    a. Have you reported this to your insurance company? (rule out duplicate property damage claims). If so, what carrier and policy number?

12. Closing

Do you understand that if you work or receive income from any other source while receiving workers' compensation benefits you must immediately report the fact of the employment or monies received to the carrier or insurance company. (Response)

ASK: Is there anything else you would like to add or clarify in this statement before I conclude the recording? (If the response is no, proceed with the closing. If the response is yes, let the subject explain and ask follow-up questions if necessary. Once you are through, repeat this statement again before proceeding).

(Subject's Name), was everything you told me true and correct to the best of your knowledge and belief? (Subject's Name), were you aware that I was recording our conversation? Did I have your permission to do so? Would you please state your name for the final time? My name is (your name). Thank you for voluntarily giving this statement.

Upon request of client obtain appropriate releases and possible photograph of subject.

PERMISSIVE USE STATEMENT

(Permission Statement of Named Insured or Spouse,
Original Permissive User (who may or may not
have been driving) or Driver -- Long Form.)

1. Usual introductory and identifying material. (See Items 1, 2 and 9, General Fact Statement, pages 22 and 23.)

2. Identify auto.

3. Who was driving at time of accident?

4. Was there express permission from named insured or spouse or anyone else to permittee or driver?

   a. If not, specifically negate such permission.
   b. If so, set out fully and in detail:

      1. What was said and/or done by the parties.
      2. Where and when the conversation or acts took place. Who was present?

   c. Was use limited:

      1. As to time, place or distance?
      2. As to purpose?

         a. Was the purpose primarily for the accomplishment of some end desired by or in the interest of the named insured or spouse? (Agency)
         b. Or, was the purpose primarily for the benefit of or in the interest of the permittee or driver? (Bailment)

      3. To include only original permittee?

   d. Or, was use unlimited?

      1. Was anything said as to purpose of or limitation on use?
      2. Had driver or permittee used auto before under these or other circumstances?

         a. Describe or negate. If so, did named insured or spouse know of such use? Any objection?

      3. To what use did named insured or spouse believe auto would be put?

   e. To what use (time, place, purpose) was auto put at time of this accident?

1. Where was permittee or driver going when accident occurred? Why?
2. Where was permittee or driver coming from when accident occurred? Why?
3. Was primary purpose of use for benefit of named insured or spouse, permittee or driver? Describe.

5. Was permission implied from named insured or spouse to permittee or driver?

   a. Recite full, minute details concerning:

      1. Exactly how permittee or driver happened to secure use of auto.
      2. What prior connection did permittee or driver have with insured's auto other than driving it.

         a. If none, so state.
         b. If any, detail fully.

      3. Any prior use of the insured's auto by permittee or driver?

         a. If none, so state.
         b. If any, full details as to permission and use, including:

            1. Permission on those occasions. Express, implied, from whom?
            2. Restrictions or limitations on use as to time, place, purpose.
            3. Actual use on these occasions.

               a. Any objection to such use by named insured or spouse.

            4. To what use (time, place, purpose) was auto put at time of this accident?

               a. Where was driver going? Why?
               b. Where was driver coming from when accident occurred? Why?
               c. Was primary purpose of use for benefit of named insured or spouse, permittee or driver? Describe.

6. Did the permission to permittee or driver come from someone other than the named insured or spouse?

   a. From whom did it come?
   b. What authority did such "other person" have to choose other users?

      1. Give complete details as to how such "other person" happened to have custody and/or control of auto.
      2. Is named insured or spouse a non-driver?

3. Was auto left in complete control and custody of such "other person"?
4. Were any limitations imposed upon such "other person" as to designation or choice of other users?

   a. Was the choice of other users left to discretion of such "other person"?
   b. Were other users to be identified or designated by named insured or spouse?
   c. If the matter was never discussed, so state.

5. Were any limitations imposed upon such "other person" as to purpose, time, place or use to which the auto was to be put? Describe.

c. Had such "other person" authorized use of the insured's auto by others on prior occasions? Explain in detail, including:

1. Whether named insured or spouse had any part in choice or designation of such other users.
2. Had user in this accident ever been so authorized? Give complete details.
3. Had named insured or spouse known of this? Any objection?

d. What use was authorized by "other person" to user involved in this accident?

1. Set out fully and in detail:

   a. What was said and/or done by the parties?
   b. Where and when conversation or acts took place. Who was present?
   c. Was use limited as to time, place, purpose?

      1. Was the purpose primarily for the accomplishment of some end desired by or in the interest of the named insured or spouse?
      2. Or, was the purpose primarily for the benefit of or in the interest of the user or the "other person"?

   d. Or, was use unlimited? Was anything said as to purpose of or limitation on use?

   e. To what use (time, place, purpose) was auto put at time of this accident?

      1. Where was user going when accident occurred? Why?
      2. Where was user coming from when accident occurred?
      3. Was primary purpose of use for benefit of named insured or spouse, "other person" or user? Describe.

   f. Identify any vehicles (make, model, and year) owned by the driver of the insured vehicle. Identify any other automobile insurance that may cover the driver.

7. Standard Closing; Signature; Initial. (See Recorded or Written Statement.)

PERMISSIVE USE STATEMENT
(Streamlined Version)

1. Usual Introduction. (See Recorded Statement or Written Statement.)

2. Identify witness and auto involved. (See General Fact Statement)

3. Who was driving at time of accident?

4. How did he happen to be driving?

    a. Who gave him permission?

        1. What authority did such person have to give it?

    b. Exactly how was his permission given?

        1. Express - what was said?
        2. Implied - what was said, done; prior course of conduct?

5. What limitations as to time, place or manner of use imposed when permission granted?

    a. Exactly what was said?
    b. If nothing said, what was prior understanding or course of conduct? Is car used regularly?

6. For what purpose was vehicle being used at time of accident?

    a. Where was driver going to and coming from?

        1. Why?

7. What vehicles does the driver personally own? What insurance company are they covered by?

8. Standard Closing; Signature; Initials. (See Recorded or Written Statement.)

POLICE OFFICER'S STATEMENT

1. Usual Introduction. (See Recorded or Written Statement.)

2. Identify officer, badge number, station.

3. How did officer happen to cover case?

4. Did officer witness accident? If so, take usual general fact statement.

5. Time of arrival at scene.

6. What did officer observe at scene?

   a. Were autos (or auto and/or pedestrian) still at scene? If so, locate and identify.
   b. Describe damage to autos. If case involved auto and pedestrian, locate and describe any marks or dents on auto and locate any autos parked at curbs.
   c. Point of impact:

      1. Were objects (autos, pedestrians) in same position as immediately after impact or had they been moved.
      2. Any physical evidence to locate point of impact?

         a. Debris: describe and locate headlight glass, blood, oil, anti-freeze, groceries, broken milk bottle, etc.
         b. Skid marks: describe and locate.

   d. Who was at scene when officer arrived?

      1. Other police? Identify.
      2. Witnesses? Identify.
      3. What did witnesses say? If statements taken, go over with officer.
      4. Tow trucks? Identify.
      5. Photographers? Identify.
      6. Any of the parties, involved?

         a. If so, did officer interview?
         b. What did parties say? Any admissions against interest?
         c. If statements were taken, go over with officer.

7. Condition of pedestrian and/or drivers.

   a. Had been drinking?

      b.   How determined? Sobriety test, smell, talk, staggering?
      c.   Physical condition other than drinking?

          1.   What inquiry alleged?
          2.   What injury apparent?

8.   Condition of vehicles:

      a.   Checked by officer?
      b.   Findings by officer: lights, brakes, horn, windows and windshield clear, etc.?

9.   Traffic controls:

      a.   Describe.
      b.   Working?

10.   Weather: Describe.

11.   Light conditions:

      a.   Describe.
      b.   If dark, what was artificial lighting?

12.   Road condition:

      a.   Describe.
      b.   Any defects?

13.   Were seat belts used?

14.   Disposition of Injured:

      a.   Where taken?
      b.   By whom?

15.   Disposition of autos:

      a.   Where taken?
      b.   Why whom?

16.   Photographs?

17.   Arrests?

18. Standard Close; Signature; Initial Errors. (See Recorded or Written Statement.)

STATEMENT OF INSURED
IN GUEST CASE

1. Usual Introduction. (See page 10 for Recorded Statement or page 11 for Written Statement.)

2. Identify witness. (See Item 2, General Fact Statement on page 22.)

3. Detailed recital of how guest(s) happened to be in auto:

    a. Events leading up to guest's entry into auto.
    b. Time elements.
    c. Drinking? Cover in detail.
    d. Had guest ridden with insured before?
       How often?

4. Negate consideration or payment of any kind to driver, or anyone else, by guest or anyone on this behalf.

5. Negate anything resembling contractual relationship.

6. Set out details of trip prior to accident; negate negligent acts or pattern of negligence through enumeration of "prudent man" acts of insured.

7. Negate any warning or objection by anyone as to manner in which auto driven.

8. Cite guest's opportunities to alight; negate any request to be allowed to alight.

9. Use of seat belts.

10. Detailed account of accident. (Refer to Items 3-12, General Fact Statement, pages 20 thru 23.)

11. Did insured realize what he was doing was negligent? (Negate any conscious indifference for safety of others).

12. Was guest aware of danger arising? Negate any warning as to the acts of negligence here involved.

13. Has guest ridden with insured since the accident? When?

14. Standard Close; Signature; Initial Errors. (See Recorded or Written Statement.)

GUEST'S EXONERATING STATEMENT
(Declaring the insured blameless or not at fault)

1. Usual Introduction and Identification Material.

2. Identify guest.

3. Detailed recital of how guests happened to be in auto:

    a. Events leading up to guest's entry into auto.
    b. Time elements.
    c. Drinking? Cover in detail.
    d. Has guest ridden with insured before?
       How often? When last?

4. Negate consideration or payment of any kind to driver, or anyone else, by guest or anyone on his behalf.

5. Negate anything resembling contractual relationship.

6. Set out details of trip prior to accident; negate negligent acts or pattern of negligence through enumeration of "prudent man" acts of insured.

7. Negate any warning or objection by guest as to manner in which auto was driven.

8. Cite guest's opportunities to alight; negate any request to be allowed to alight.

9. Use of seat belts.

10. Detailed account of accident. (See items 3-12, General Fact Statement, pages 22 thru 25.)

11. Was guest aware of danger arising?

12. Did guest know whether his driver was aware of danger?

13. Did he warn driver? Why not? (Negate any warning as to the acts of negligence here involved.)

14. Characterize insured's driving as careful and proper.

15. Would guest ride with insured again? Why?

16. State the following if applicable:

    "At all times during the trip Mr. (insured) was driving properly. He obeyed all traffic signs and signals; did not exceed any speed limits; and kept his speed down according to traffic conditions, road conditions and weather conditions. At no time during the trip did I or anyone in the car object to the manner in which Mr. (insured) drove the car."

17. Standard Close; Signature; Initial Errors. (See Recorded or Written Statement.)

18. (Note: Consider advisability of securing Medical and Employment Authorizations.)

MINOR BODILY INJURY STATEMENT
(Parent -- Guardian or "Well-Being" Statement
(To assist an Adjuster when gathering facts to
use in settling a Minor's B.I. claim)

1. Usual Introduction and Identifying Material. (See General Fact Statement)

2. Identify parent(s) giving statement.

3. Relation to the injured minor. (Natural parent, guardian, adopted, etc.).

4. Parent's marital status. (Widow, divorced, etc.)

5. Name, age, marital status of the minor.

6. Child does or does not reside with the parent (or parents).

7. Very brief description of accident. (Include date, time, place, city and state, etc.)

8. Describe injury to minor, if any.

9. Medical treatment given, if any:

    a. By whom? Name, address.
    b. What treatment? Describe briefly.

10. Parent's observations of child's behavior and physical condition at present time:

    a. Parent is satisfied that minor is normal and has no ill effects and none are anticipated.
    b. No returns to Doctor are anticipated. Or, if they are anticipated, state why and show it doesn't change parent's opinion of child's normalcy, etc.
    c. Expenses incurred? Brief details.
    d. Any anticipated expenses? Details.

11. Expression of parent's desire to settle the claim.

12. Standard Close; Signature; Initial Errors. (See Recorded or Written Statement.)

PIP STATEMENT
(Guest Driving Insured's Vehicle)

FROM: Insured

1. Introduction (See Recorded or Written Statement)

2. Identify Insured:

    Name, age, address, phone number, marital status, spouse's name, children's names and ages, occupation, employer, social security number, relative's name and address.

3. Identify automobile in question by make, model, year, color, license number, etc.

4. Who was driving vehicle at the time of the accident or incident?

5. Was driver living with insured at the time when policy taken out?

    a. If no, when did he/she move in?
    b. If yes, why wasn't driver listed on policy?

6. What is name and address of insurance agent who can verify information?

7. Obtain names of individuals who can deny or confirm the claimant's address information.

    a. Landlord
    b. Roommates
    c. Mail
    d. Friends
    e. Acquaintance
    f. Neighborhood sources

8. Why does driver claim he lived at residence during the time of the accident?

9. What is the actual address of claimant?

10. Names of subject's which can verify claimant's real address.

    a. Relatives
    b. Friends/Boy/Girlfriend
    c. Employer
    d. Co-employees
    i. Letters
    e. Neighborhood sources
    f. Car registration
    g. Driver's license
    h. Applications

11. Does the claimant own any vehicle that you are aware of?

12. Where does he keep this vehicle?

13. How did driver come in possession of the vehicle?

14. What vehicle or vehicles does the driver personally own?

    a. What insurance company insures said vehicles?

15. Closing:

    a. For recorded statement refer to Closing Statement on page 10.
    b. For written statements have interviewee "initial" each page, and include on last page acknowledgement, "I have read the above report of _____ pages and it is true and correct to the best of my knowledge and belief." Have interviewee also check to be certain that all errors have been initialed.

PIP STATEMENT
(Driver of Insured's Vehicle)

FROM: Driver

1. Introduction (See Recorded or Written Statement)

2. Identify Driver:

    Name, age, address, phone number, marital status, spouse's name, children's names and ages, occupation, employer, social security number, relative's name and address.

3. Identify automobile in question by make, model, year, color, license number, etc.

4. Does subject own his own vehicle?

5. If yes, obtain information on vehicle, make, model, year, color, license number, etc.

6. Identify driver's insurance carrier on personal vehicle.

7. Where does driver live?

8. Where did driver live at the time of the accident?

9. How long has he lived there?

10. When did he move in?

11. Name of subjects who can verify subject's residency.

    a. Relatives
    b. Friends/Boy/Girlfriend
    c. Employer
    d. Co-employees
    e. Driver's license
    f. Car registration
    g. Neighborhood sources
    h. Mail

12. How did driver come in possession of vehicle?

13. Where was he going or coming from?

14. What vehicle(s) does the driver personally own?

    a. Name of insurance company covering vehicle(s).

15. Closing:

   a. For recorded statement refer to Closing Statement on page 10.

   b. For written statements have interviewee "initial" each page, and include on last page acknowledgement, "I have read the above report of _____ pages and it is true and correct to the best of my knowledge and belief." Have interviewee also check to be certain that all errors have been initialed.

   (BI Claimant, obtain Medical and Employment Authorizations.) After statement, it may be requested that you obtain Medical and Employee Wage Authorizations.

CHAPTER 4 – GENERAL LIABILITY

SLIP/FALL STATEMENT
(Fall Down Cases)

1. Introduction (See Recorded or Written Statement)

2. Identify claimant:

    a. Name, age, address, marital status, phone, etc.
    b. Occupation and address, phone, salary, etc.
    c. Other insurance benefits -- names of companies and benefits. (Exclude from s/s).

3. Why claimant at scene:

    a. Guest? Details of visit.
    b. Licensee? Details of purpose of visit.
    c. Invitee? Details of purpose of visit.
    d. Trespasser? Details of entrance upon the premises.
    e. A minor? Attractive nuisance doctrine possibilities.
    f. Landlord - Tenant relationship.
    g. Employer - Employee relationship.

4. Location of accident:

    a. Common stairway or private?
    b. Sidewalk? Public or private?
    c. Apartment building and leases, if any, involved?
    d. How often was claimant there before? Last specific date of visit?

5. Defects:

    a. Negate, if none.
    b. Did claimant see of know of defect. Describe defect and location.
    c. Was defect present last time claimant was there? Date.
    d. Did defect cause accident?
    e. Did insured know of defect? If so, when? What did he do about correcting it or protecting others from its potential danger?

6. Lighting.

a. Artificial: Adequate? Type? Number and positions in relation to point of fall down?
   b. Natural: Enough? Not enough?
   c. Did lighting show up defects?
   d. Did lack of light cause accident?

7. Other important facts:

   a. Bannister there? Was it used?
   b. Type of shoes worn? Type soles? Type heels?
   c. Claimant in a hurry? If so, why?
   d. Claimant carrying anything? What? How or in what manner?
   e. Admissions made by insured and claimant at time of accident? Describe.

8. Precise location of fall:

   a. Exact step claimant fell on?
   b. Exact spot in walk claimant fell?

9. Description of fall:

   a. Feet slip out from under?
   b. Fell forward?
   c. Twisted ankle?
   d. Other possible ways claimant fell.
   e. How did claimant land?

10. Injury sustained:

    a. Did defect cause injury? Describe claimant's symptoms and complaints in detail. Identity of claimant's doctor, hospital, type of treatment given and cost to date.

    b. Did claimant ever injure this part of body before? History of past injury, names of hospitals he was in, names and addresses of doctors who rendered any services, etc.

11. Identify all witnesses:

    a. Impartial?
    b. Bias? Accompanying claimant?
    c. After witnesses.

12. Closing:

a. See Usual Recorded Statement Closing
b. For written statements have interviewee "initial" each page, and include on last page acknowledgement, "I have read the above report of _____ pages and it is true and correct to the best of my knowledge and belief." Have interviewee also check to be certain that all errors have been initialed.

(BI Claimant, obtain Medical and Employment Authorizations.) After statement, it may be requested that you obtain Medical and Employee Wage Authorizations.

DOG BITE STATEMENT

The following statement guideline has been designed for dog-bite cases, but can easily be made applicable to other animal attack cases. Statutes and ordinances vary significantly in imposing liability for dog-bites. Most states make owners completely liable for the actions of their dogs, but some make an exception for the first bite. Liability may be eliminated or decreased if the claimant had no legal right to be on the premises or if he provoked the animal. Before continuing your investigation of a dog-bite case, you should become fully acquainted with the appropriate law(s) in your jurisdiction.

1. Introduction (See Recorded or Written Statement)

2. Personal data on insured (homeowner):

    a. Name, address, and home phone number of insured.
    b. Type of work, where employed, and length of employment.
    c. Name of spouse.
    d. Spouse's type of work, where employed, length of employment.

3. Description of Incident:

    Ask the interviewee to describe in his own words the events involved in the incident. He should describe the reason for the claimant's presence, the claimant's familiarity with the animal, and any form of control being exerted over the animal at the time. Then ask any of the following questions which you need to get a full picture of the incident.

4. Circumstances Surrounding Incident:

    a. Exact time and location of incident.
    b. Animal's species, breed, size, color, and age.
    c. If the insured owns the animal, how long has he owned it? If not owned by the insured, who does own it?
    d. Name and occupation of the claimant.

5. Reason for Claimant's Presence:

    a. Was the claimant on premises for business reasons? (Appointment, soliciting, etc.).
    b. If not, why was he there? (Guest, relative, etc.)

6. Provocation:

    a. Was the animal in any way provoked by the claimant? Did he, for instance, strike, threaten, or make a sudden movement in front of the animal?

b. Were other animals involved in the incident? Were they running loose or under control?
c. Did the claimant interfere with them while they were fighting or romping?

7. Propensity (Tendencies or Inclination):

    a. General condition and health of the animal?
    b. Are all shots up to date?
    c. Animal's temperament and general disposition. (Check with neighbors.)
    d. Was the animal ever involved in a previous incident?
    e. Have previous complaints been made against this animal?
    f. Was our insured aware of these complaints or of any other indications of the animal's vicious propensity? If so, did he take any steps to war or protect the public (fences, signs, etc.)?

8. Restraint of Animal by Insured:

    a. At the time of the incident, was the insured exerting any type of control or restraint over the animal?
    b. Was the insured in violation of any ordinances (licensing, leash laws, etc.)?
    c. Was the animal properly enclosed, caged, chained, or tied? Had it escaped from any sort of restraint?

9. Additional Factors Affecting Liability:

    a. Had the claimant been on premises before? If so, was he aware of the animal's presence? Of its temperament?
    b. Had the claimant ever been made aware in any other way of the animal's presence or temperament?
    c. Did the claimant try to avoid the animal?
    d. Was the dog in heat or with puppies?

10. Damages:

    a. Describe the injury in detail.
    b. Was the health department notified of the incident? If so, did they take any action? Was the animal checked for rabies? Were any laboratory tests made?
    c. Describe the treatment rendered; include names of doctors and hospitals.
    d. Did the claimant lose any time from work? If so, identify name of employer, wage rate, time lost, etc.
    e. Does any sort of disability remain? Are there any scars?

12. Closing:

    a. For recorded statement refer to Recorded Statement Closing
    b. For written statements have interviewee "initial" each page, and include on last page acknowledgement, "I have read the above report of _____ pages and It is true and correct to the best of my knowledge and belief." Have interviewee also check to be certain that all errors have

been initialed.

(BI Claimant, obtain Medical and Employment Authorizations.) After statement, it may be requested that you obtain Medical and Employee Wage Authorizations.

CHAPTER 5 - HOMEOWNERS THEFT / BURGLARY

PROPERTY THEFT STATEMENT

1. Introduction (See Recorded or Written Statement)

2. Personal Data on Insured:

   a. Name, address, and home phone number of insured.
   b. Type of work, where employed, and length of employment.
   c. Name of spouse.
   d. Spouse's type of work, where employed, and length of employment.

3. Description of Incident:

   Ask the insured to describe in his own words each of the following: the stolen object, the time and location of the theft, and how entry was gained (where applicable). Then ask any of the following which you need to get a full picture of the incident.

4. Circumstances Surrounding Theft:

   a. Location from which property was taken.
   b. Who left it there?
   c. When and why was it left there?
   d. When was property last seen?
   e. How was property taken?
   f. By whom and when was loss discovered?
   g. Where was insured at time of loss?
   h. Did stolen property have any business use? If so, what?
   i. Any unusual occurrences prior to loss.

5. Structure Burglarized:

   a. If house burglarized:

      1. Was dwelling the insured's home? If not, why was he there?
      2. Type of dwelling.
      3. Number of residents, their relation to insured.
      4. Were all doors and windows locked?
      5. How was entry gained?
      6. Any damage to dwelling? Are repairs needed?

7. Who has access to building?

b. If garage or other outbuilding burglarized:

1. Location of building.
2. Were all doors and windows locked?
3. How was entry gained?
4. Are repairs needed?
5. Who has access to building?

c. If apartment burglarized:

1. On which floor is apartment located?
2. Number of apartments on same floor; number in building.
3. Number of entrances to apartment; number in building.
4. Were doors and windows of apartment locked?
5. How was entry gained?
6. Any damage to apartment?
7. Who has keys to apartment?
8. Any security system?

6. Police Report:

a. Which police department wrote report?
b. Case number.
c. Name of investigating officer.
d. Time at which police were called.
e. Was investigation performed at scene?
f. Did detectives follow-up?
g. Were evidence tests performed, e.g. fingerprints, etc.?
h. Were neighbors interviewed?
i. Other recent burglaries in area?
j. Was complete inventory taken?

7. Loss Evaluation:

a. For all items, establish: brand, serial number, cost, place and date of purchase, and estimated current value.
b. Are receipts available?
c. Is this inventory complete?
d. Has a thorough search been made for all items?
e. Have all items been reported to police?
f. Does insured own all items?
g. If not, who does?

    h.   Any of missing items financed?
    i.   If so, with whom, what account number?
    j.   Any other insured on items? If so, name of carrier, policy number.

8. Insurance History:

    a.   Has insured had prior theft losses?
    b.   Time and circumstances of such losses.
    c.   Name and carrier at that time, policy number.

9. Closing:

    a.   For recorded statement refer to Closing Statement on page 10.
    b.   For written statements have interviewee "initial" each page, and include on last page acknowledgement, "I have read the above report of _____ pages and it is true and correct to the best of my knowledge and belief." Have interviewee also check to be certain that all errors have been initialed.

THEFT OUTLINE - ALLSTATE

1. This is (Your Name) interviewing (witness name) at (location of interview). Today's date is (date) and the time is (time). This interview concerns a (type of loss) on (date of loss) at (location of loss).

2. Would you please state your full name, spelling the last?

3. Are you aware we are recording this interview?

4. Is the recording being made with your permission?

5. (Mr./Mrs.) What is your age and date of birth?

6. (Mr./Mrs.) What is your social security number?

7. (Mr./Mrs.) Are you married? What is your (husband's/wife's name?)

8. How many people live in home? Names, relationship?

9. Where are you employed? How long have you been employed by _____?

10. Is your (husband/wife) employed?

11. Are you the owner of (location of loss)? When did you purchase (location of loss)?

12. Where did you live prior to living at (location of loss)?

13. Do you have any other name?

14. Can you tell me the date and time of the theft?

15. Can you tell me where you were at the time of the theft? Where was your family?

16. Who notified you of the theft? How were you notified?

17. Do you own any other property? Where?

18. Do you own any pets? Where were they at the time of the theft?

19. Who was the last one in the building?

20. Who called police?

21. Were there signs of forced entry?

22. How did burglars get in?

23. Did you lock the building when you left?

24. Who had keys to the building?

25. What type of cars do you own?

26. Have you ever had any prior thefts?

27. Do you have any other insurance? Special insurance?

28. Is your home up for sale?

29. Do you have a mortgage on the property? With whom? Are payments current?

30. Have you ever been arrested for committing a criminal act?

31. Did you operate any type of business in the building?

32. Let's go over the list of stolen items!

    A. Where, when purchased?
    B. Where was the item located in your home?
    C. How much then?
    D. How much now?
    E. How did you pay for item? Cash? Charge? Check? Time payments?

MISCELLANEOUS QUESTIONS

i. Can you think of anything that we have not discussed?

ii. (Mr./Mrs.) Have you understood all of my questions?

iii. Is there anything you would care to add or change concerning this interview?

iv. Have all of your answers been true and correct?

v. Please state your name and address to end this recording.

MISSING PROPERTY STATEMENT GUIDE

1. Name?
2. Address?
3. Age and occupation?
4. How long at this address?
5. Prior address?
6. Marital status?
7. Wife's (husband's) name, age and occupation?
8. Any other member of household or residents?
9. Their name, age and occupation?
10. Date and time a theft loss occurred at your home?
11. How loss was discovered?
12. Who discovered loss and where?
13. Activities prior to loss?
14. Condition of premises prior to loss--door and windows locked?
15. Description of exactly what you first noticed when loss was discovered?
16. How was entry made?
17. What evidence of forcible entry?
18. After discovery of loss what did you do?
19. Policy agency notified?
20. When and were notified?
21. Ownership of property taken?
22. Detailed description of property, i.e., location, age, purchased price, I.D. number, make, etc.
23. Location of property when taken? Who placed it there?
24. Photographs of property location.
25. Age of property--when acquired?
26. Where acquired?
27. Purchase price?
28. Serial numbers?

29. Identifying marks?
30. If money, the amount and explanation as to the knowledge of amounts--denominations?
31. If itemization of above property the same as given to police?
32. If not, why not--supplementary inventory to police?
33. What police investigation was made?
34. If no evidence of forcible entry, when was property last seen?
35. How did you discover property missing?
36. When was property discovered missing?
37. Activities from the time the property was last seen, i.e., shopping gardening, cleaning house, doing dishes, etc.?
38. Anything else discovered out of the ordinary, moved about, upset, etc.?
39. Any neighbors have similar problems?
40. Who would have had access to the property (household help, animals, baby-sitter, party guests, real estate people, etc.)?
41. Ever had any other thefts or claims similar to this?
42. When and where?
43. How long have you been insured with company?
44. Who before, name of agent and company?
45. Do you have any other insurance policies, credit loans, possible insurance coverage? Forward copy of contact.

To be used as a guide for narrative and recorded report statement taking.

CHAPTER 6 -AUTO THEFT

GENERAL AUTO THEFT STATEMENT OUTLINE

In preparation of recorded statement:

Before returning on recorder socialize briefly with the subject. Advise subject that they will need their driver's license number, previous addresses, names and addresses of hospitals, doctors and therapists. Also, subject should be prepared to identify prescription drugs and frequency of use, prior employers' names and addresses and information related to any previous insurance claims. Request that the subject gather the information before you turn on the recorder. Give the subject a general overview of what to expect during the interview.

Before turning on the recorder determine if the subject is on any medication. Make sure that this medication will not effect the subject's ability to give an accurate statement.

Introduction to Statement: **Turn on Recorder**

Today's date is _____. My name is (your name) and I am employed with Claims Resource Incorporated and represent (name of insurance company). I am at (the location where you are taking the statement from). I am interviewing (name of subject) who was involved in a workers' compensation accident. (Name of claimant), are you aware that I am recording this conversation: (Response). Do I have your permission to do so? (Response).

1. Personal History

    a. What is your full name and please spell your last name?
       1. Do you have any alias or nicknames?
       2. What is your maiden name?
       3. Have you ever had your name changed?
    b. What is your current address and how long have you been living at this location?
    c. Do you own or rent? Who is responsible for the care and upkeep of your home/lawn?
    d. What is your home phone number and an emergency phone number where you can be reached?
    e. What is your previous address? Did you rent or own?
    f. What is your date and place of birth?
    g. What is your social security number and driver's license number?
    h. Do you wear corrective lens? glasses/contacts
    i. Do you smoke?
    j. What is the last grade you completed (high school, technical, trade school, or college?)
    k. Are you married? If so, what is your spouse's name?
    l. Do you have any dependents? (If yes name(s) and age(s). (Do they live at home?)
    m. What is the name and address of your closest living relative?

n. Have you ever been convicted of a crime? (If yes, date(s), location,, charges, involved in a work release program).

3. Current Employment

   a. What is the name and address of your current employer
   b. How long have you been employed with your current employer?
   c. What is your job title?
   d. What is your working schedule-from what time to what time? What days each week?
   e. How do you usually get to work?

4. Residential and Vehicle Information

   a. How many cars do you own at the present time?
      List all:
      make/model/color/tag numbers/INSURANCE CARRIERS
   b. Do you have anyone else living with you? If yes identify vehicles owned.
   c. Do you have any renters? If yes identify vehicles
   d. Where do you park each car? Describe parking location.

5. Stolen Vehicle/Loss

   a. Identify the vehicle stolen.
      1. year
      2. make/model/color
      3. VIN (Vehicle Identification Number?)
      4. mileage
      5. extra equipment?
         a. CB
         b. CD changer
         c. Post factory Stereo system
         d. ALARM? If so what type?
            1. Any theft warranty/guarantee?
            2. Was it on? if so how does subject explain theft?
               a. Was there an ignition disabling feature in alarm package?
               b. Have any other break-ins or theft occurred while this alarm was on? If so was it reported to the police? When, where and what date(s)
            3. If not on why not?
      6. Tag number and State of issue
      7. Any Stickers or Decals? Description and location.
      8. Describe dents, dings, scrapes, scratches, broken glass, missing parts or any other markings.
   b. What was this car used for? work? if so what is distance?
   c. Where is it normally parked?
   d. How many sets of keys are there to this vehicle? Any missing?

- e. Who ALL drives this or has access to it?
- f. Who used the car last, immediately prior to theft?
- g. List all other possible drivers
    - a. spouse, children, friends, co-employees, etc..
- h. Where and when was car last seen? By whom?
    - a. When was gas last put in vehicle? Any receipt?
- i. What if any personal property was inside the car - full description
    1. Brand, serial number, cost, place, date of purchase, method of payment and estimated current value.
    2. Are receipts available?
    3. Is the inventory sent to the Insurance Company complete?
    4. What inventory was identified in the police report? Is there any different between the two if so why? and have the police been re-contacted to update police report?
    5. Has a thorough search for the items been made?
    6. Does the insured own all the items?
    7. Any of the missing items financed? If so with whom and what account numbers?
    8. Any other insurance on items? Is so, name of carrier, policy number
- j. What was in the glove box? Trunk?
- k. Was this cars registration current?
- l. Was ignition locked when car was left? Where doors locked? Windows locked?
- m. Were there any keys hidden in or outside the car?
- n. Do you have other transportation available to you?
    1. Second car?
    2. Car Pool possibility
    3. Friends, co-worker in area?
    4. Taxi, Buses?
- o. When will alternate transportation be required?
- p. What arrangements have been made?

6. Incident/Loss

- a. Where were you going at the time you discovered the loss? Or where were you coming from?
- b. Was this a planned trip or a normal everyday event?
- c. Did you plan to leave at this time? If so what plans where made? Anything special or out of the ordinary?
    1. On vacation leaving town? Had Hotel reservations etc.?
- d. Do you have any idea who might have stolen the car?
- e. Do the police have any suspects?
- f. How was the car broken into? Any keys missing?
- g. Who first discovered the car was missing?
    1. What time was this?
    2. What date?

      e.   What did you do next? Call Police? Call insurance company?
      f.   Was the vehicle recovered? If so who found it?
          a.   how were you notified?
          b.   Was there any personal property still in the vehicle?
      g.   Did you speak to any neighbors?
      h.   Had anyone seen or heard anything relating to the loss, i.e. neighbor heard glass break at ? time, etc?
      i.   Was anyone with you or outside at the time you discovered your vehicle missing? Obtain description name and address of witnesses.
      j.   What was your reaction? What did you think of at that moment?
      k.   What were you doing just prior to finding the loss.

8. Police
    a.   Who called the police?
    b.   What time was this done?
    c.   What time did the Police arrive?
    d.   What Police Agency responded?
        a.   Police Officers Name
        b.   Badge Number?
    c.   Case Number
    e.   Who filled out or was interviewed by the officer for official report?
    f.   Did you hand write your own statement?
    g.   How much time did you take to prepare a statement to the police?
    h.   Was a list of the personal items in the vehicle given at the time the police officer arrived?
    i.   How much time did you have to gather these items?
    j.   Did the Police perform an investigation at the scene?
    k.   Did detectives follow-up?
    l.   Were any evidence tests performed, i.e., finger prints, etc.?
    m.   Did the police interview neighbors?
    n.   Other recent Burglaries in area?
    o.   Was a complete inventory taken?

12. Post Incident Activities
    a.   Did you eventual leave for your original destination once the police and Insurance company were notified? Did you go to work?
    b.   What transportation did you use?
    c.   What time did you eventually leave?
    d.   Has any of the personal property been replaced?
        1.   Do you have the receipts for those items replaced by you?

13. History of Vehicle

    a.   When was vehicle purchased?
    b.   From Whom? Full name and address

  c. Cost?
  d. Any Trade-In? Is so describe trade-in and allowance.
  e. Do you have a copy of the sales contract? Could you get a copy?
  f. Method of Payment?
   1. Down payment
   2. financed? through who? terms?
   3. Monthly payments?
   4. Are payments up to date?
   5. What is your balance
   6. Will your insurance cover your amount owed on vehicle?
   7. Is insurance included in your financing?
   8. Monthly cost of Insurance?
  g. How long have you had Insurance on your vehicle?
  h. Was there any prior insurance coverage on this vehicle with another carrier?
  i. Have any prior claims for loss associated with this car been made to another Insurance Company?
  j. Have you had any prior reported theft losses? If so what carrier and Police was this reported to?
  k. Was normal maintenance performed as suggested by Owner's Manual?
  l. Who has performed maintenance on this vehicle? Name and address of Dealer, Garage and Mechanic.
  m. What was the date of the last service?
  n. What service was performed? Amount?
  o. Any more recent mechanical/cosmetic problems with vehicle?
  p. Was this car ever in an Accident? If so where were Mechanical and Body repairs made?
   1. What carrier was claim submitted to?
   2. Was a police report filed? If so where and what date?
  q. Was any new item recently purchased for the car? If so, what and where is it now? Car bra, stereo, seat covers, etc?
   1. Any receipts for items?

14. Prior Insurance Claims
  a. Have you ever had any type of theft claim before? If so, provide details.
  b. Have you ever had any other type of claim(s) against an insurance company?

Statement Closing

ASK: Is there anything else you would like to add or clarify in this statement before I conclude the recording? (If the response if no, proceed with the closing. If the response is yes, let the subject explain and ask follow-up questions if necessary. Once you are through, repeat this statement again before proceeding).

(Subject's Name), was everything you told me true and correct to the best of your knowledge and belief? (Subject's Name), were you aware that I was recording our conversation? Did I have your permission to do so? Would you please state your name for the final time? My name is (your name). Thank you for voluntarily giving this statement.

CHAPTER 7 - FIRE STATEMENT

STATEMENTS FROM DISCOVERER(S) OF FIRE, MEDIA REPORTER(S) AND OTHER PERSONS WHO EYEWITNESSED THE FIRE

1) Name, home & business addresses & phone numbers
2) Age, occupation & marital status
3) Exact time and place where fire discovered
4) Color of flames
5) Color of smoke
6) Unusual odors at fire scene
7) Explosion or other noise
8) Rapidity & direction fire spread
9) How attention drawn to fire
10) Location & activity of observer at time of discovery
11) Activity observed just prior to discovery
12) How, where and to whom fire was reported
13) Observer's activity after fire's discovery
14) Vehicles leaving and arriving at scene
15) Persons leaving and at scene
16) Description of all persons at scene before arrival of firemen
17) Description of all persons at scene from arrival of firemen to time observer left scene
18) Weather conditions
19) How observer thinks fire started
20) Names & addresses of persons who may know about the fire or property burned
21) Other fires in same neighborhood
22) Conversations with persons in crowd at scene of fire
23) Whether any threats or statements are made to the discoverer by the insured or others
24) Number of other fires "discovered" by the witness
25) Other matters
26) Did subject ever discuss his private life: marital problems, financial
27) (Insured's) subject's employment, daily activity
28) Was anything done on the part of subject differently on the date of the fire than his normal routine
29) Where were cars parked (usual position?)
30) Were family members around, if not why?
31) Other witness or those that may have knowledge of insured's activities before fire
32) How long did it take until insured came out
33) How did he act, what did he say
34) Did he move any valuable objects out of house prior to fire?
35) Insured's character(?)
36) Did he live full time at residence

STATEMENTS (UNSWORN) FROM INSURED(S), OWNER(S), LANDLORD(S), TENANT(S) AND OCCUPANT(S) OF BURNED STRUCTURE

1) Name, address & telephone numbers, social security number
2) Occupation, employer, age, marital status, family members
3) When & from whom insured property was purchased; purchase price
4) Location at time of fire
5) If eye witnessed fire, include questions for eyewitnesses See: "Statements from Discoverer(s) of fire, Media Reporter(s), and other persons who Eye witnessed the Fire"
6) How notified of fire
7) Persons present when notified
8) When and where notified
9) Who provided notice of fire
10) Details provided in notice of fire
11) Activity when notice received
12) Activities before notice or discovery of fire
13) When last at premises
14) Building locked when last left
15) Who has keys to premises
16) Names & addresses of all persons having ownership interest in burned structure
17) Names & addresses of all persons who had been living in burned structure
18) Last person(s) on premises before fire
19) Repairs needed or completed before fire
20) Names & addresses of repairmen
21) Age of burned structure
22) Occupancy/vacancy/turnover rate
23) Insured property ever offered for sale
24) Any flammable liquids or substances in or near structure
25) Names & addresses of all tenants, landlords & owners of property in vicinity of burned structure
26) Names & addresses of all witnesses or other persons who may have any knowledge about the fire or insured premises
27) Previous fire losses or other insurance claims
28) All previous insurers
29) Past residences
30) Employment and occupation history
31) Names & addresses of all businesses owned or operated by insured(s)
32) Business licenses or registrations of insured
33) Financial status of business ventures of insured
34) Whether insured's business is current in filing annual fees required by local, state or federal governments
35) Past bankruptcy by insured
36) Whether any problems with customers, employees or others
37) Description of all business & personal vehicles owned or operated; lien holders on the vehicles
38) Sources of income & assets

39) Accountant or bookkeeper
40) Bank accounts & other financial information
41) Description of contents destroyed by fire
42) Personal property & irreplaceable items saved by fire
43) Whether insurance policy burned in fire
44) Location of pets or other animals of insured(s) at time of fire
45) Theories on cause of fire; how fire started
46) Any photos, drawings, blueprints, or diagrams of property before it burned
47) Litigation history of insured, both civil and criminal
48) Previous policy cancellations
49) Fire alarm or fire prevention systems in building
50) Photographs of building before and after fire
51) Who may have set the fire
52) Type of material used to start fire
53) When fire started
54) Other matters

STATEMENTS FROM NEIGHBORS AND PERSONS WHO WORK OR RESIDE IN VICINITY OF FIRE

1) Name, address & telephone number
2) How long at present address
3) Known insured(s) how long
4) Reputation of insured(s) in community
5) Insured(s) previous residences & other property owned
6) Any problems with insured(s)
7) How they became aware of fire
8) Person(s) who discovered fire, turned in alarm
9) Time fire first observed
10) If eye witnessed fire, include questions for eyewitnesses- See: "Statements from Discoverer of Fire, Media Reporter(s), and other persons who eye witnessed the fire"
11) Any unusual activities by owner(s) or occupant(s) of insured property before or after fire
12) Personal property and inventory removed from premises before and after fire
13) Visitors to insured premises before fire
14) Vehicles parked at or near insured premises before fire
15) Any persons or vehicles observed leaving scene just before fire
16) Opinion as to how fire started
17) Who all has discussed fire or talked about it
18) Any other fires in neighborhood
19) Whether insured(s) had other fires, insurance claims or property damages
20) Location of other buildings and property owned by insured
21) Whether police ever visited insured(s) before fire
22) Any financial or marital problems of insured(s)
23) Occupation, sources of income & debts of insured(s)
24) Business associates and competitors of insured(s)
25) Unusual business hours
26) Pets or other animals owned by insured(s) & their location at time of fire
27) Conversations with insured(s) since fire
28) Who all may have any knowledge of the fire, the burned structure or the insured(s); and their addresses
29) Friends and acquaintances of insured and their addresses
30) Other matters

STATEMENTS FROM FIREMEN, FIRE MARSHAL & POLICE OFFICERS

1) Name, address & phone numbers of fire/police person(s) providing statement(s)
2) Time, day of week and date when fire was reported; how fire reported
3) Identity of person reporting the fire
4) When & how reporter of fire learned of fire
5) Weather conditions, including those that delay arrival of apparatus
6) Man-made barriers that impede arrival of apparatus
7) Vehicles leaving the scene
8) Individuals leaving the scene on foot
9) Time of arrival at scene; first firemen at scene
10) General appearance & extent of the fire on arrival
11) Windows and doors covered, locked on arrival
12) Exact location of fire or area of most intense burning
13) Color of smoke flame
14) Any explosives, explosions or unusual sounds at fire scene
15) Unusual odors
16) Means of entry; whether forced entry required; first entry by whom
17) Indications of multiple, separate, unconnected fires, for example similar combustibles at several locations throughout a room
18) Abnormally rapid fire spread
19) How long and intensely fire burned
20) Measures taken to spread or accelerate burning: streamers or trailers, holes in wall and ceilings, interior doors propped open, containers or other indications of flammable liquids
21) Unusual location of the fire(s)
22) Remnants of fire sets: matches, candles, rags, paper and other delaying devices
23) The absence of those items normally associated with the type and use of the facility
24) In dwelling fires, household articles missing or outside the dwelling
25) In mercantile or industrial fires, absence of stock, fixtures, or machinery
26) Fire stop facilities tampered with or damaged
27) Fixed fire protection systems shut off or damaged
28) Obstacles blocking fire department entry
29) Burning intensified when water was applied or if reflashing occurred
30) Functioning status of energy systems and appliances in structure
31) Whether measurements or drawings made of fire scene
32) Dress of owner or occupants of burned structure
33) Familiar faces, eager helper, and unusual acting individual
34) Building in need of obvious repair
35) Building location undesirable
36) Names or description of all persons present at scene
37) Description of vehicles & crowd at scene
38) Where was owner when contacted
39) Opinion and cause of point(s) of origin

40) Comments made by spectators or neighbors
41) Other fires in same neighborhood
42) Explanation of on scene activities and matters in their reports, including names and addresses of all persons interviewed, equipment used to contain and extinguish the fire, and the time of burning before the alarm and before arrival at the scene
43) Whether any arrests were made near the fire scene on the date of the fire
44) Past criminal record, if any, of the insured
45) Whether state or federal governments may prosecute anyone as a result of the fire
46) Name and addresses of suspects, informants & witnesses
47) Present location & person having custody of photographs and other evidence obtained at fire scene
48) Whether previously testified as expert witnesses on fire cause and origin
49) Fingerprints, footprints, or toe prints
50) Any false alarms
51) Housing/Health Code Violations
52) Other matters

STATEMENT FROM INSURANCE AGENT

1) Name, address & telephone number of agent(s)
2) How long known insured(s)
3) Past employment and occupation history of insured(s)
4) Whether agent solicited insurance business of insured(s)
5) Extent of agent's knowledge of risk
6) Date risk was first underwritten; new or renewal policy
7) Dates of all amendments & increases in coverage
8) Whether agent had seen, inspected or photographed insured premises before issuing binder
9) Description of prior losses and insurance claims of insured(s), including when, where, and cause of each
10) Names & addresses of previous insurance agents and insurance companies of insured(s)
11) Insurance provided to insured other than fire coverage
12) Names & addresses of all insurance companies having any type of coverage for the insured
13) Whether insured or agent suggested limits of coverage for burned property
14) Whether insured had requested increase(s) in policy limits before property
15) Whether insured or agent completed the blanks on the application for fire insurance coverage
16) Whether insured signed or notarized the application for fire insurance coverage
17) Whether agent knows of any false statements in application for fire insurance coverage
18) Names of persons known to agent to have knowledge of financial status of insured(s)
19) Names of all persons known to agent to have any knowledge of the fire or burned structure; and their addresses
20) Time agent first learned of fire
21) Persons providing notice of fire to agent, with details of notice
22) Conversations between agent and insured before policy issued or binder given; particularly whether insured asked about fire losses or unusual coverages before the fire
23) Any problems in collecting premiums
24) Whether insured property was vacant when policy initially issued, when policy was renewed, or at any time after initial binder issued
25) Whether agent even inspected, examined or photographed the insured property; if so, dates and observations at premises
26) Whether insured property ever appraised; if so, when and by whom
27) Other matters

CHAPTER 8 - CASE STUDIES

The following is a compilation of various cases where statements were taken as part of the investigation. These statements were used to document the facts of a case as reported by the parties involved or witnesses. They were taken to clarify a matter and to document the incident while the information is still fresh in the mind of the person being interviewed. The report samples are based on my own reporting format and yours or your company may prefer the reporting in a different format. I routinely take photographs of each person interviewed and accident or incident locations. In accident cases, I take picture from each driver's perspective as well as any other pertinent matter. Most pictures are taken with my smart phone. Some cases involving fine details should be photographed with a high resolution digital camera.

CASE I – PREMINUM FRAUD – FALSE GARAGING

Mrs. Santiago was in the back seat of a vehicle driven by her daughter. Her son Christian was seated in the front passenger's seat. The daughter was driving a car insured by her father. The car was reportedly left at his ex-wife's house while he traveled to Washington on a business trip. He claimed he drive to Kissimmee and had his family take him to the airport and they brought the car back to Kissimmee while he was away. He indicated that anyone at the house had permission to use the car while he was away. The adjuster handling the claim saw that Mr. Ramero had two cars and was the only listed driver on both cars. He insured both cars stating that they were garaged at his Tampa residence. Since Mr. Ramero could not drive two cars at the same time and had no other listed drivers, his insurance on the second car was greatly discounted. Many times insurance can be purchase online, making acts like this go undetected until something major goes wrong. For an adjuster, the two cars are a "red flag" and the newly licensed driver operating the car also fits similar acts of fraud.

As you read the case, I approached this investigation thinking that the car was most likely always in Kissimmee and never in Tampa. I was prepared to get the truth from the teenage driver, however when Mr. Ramero arrived, I spoke to him briefly and stated that I would need proof of his airline ticket and out of town travel. He clearly knew the cat was out of the bag and I offered him an opportunity to come clean. Lying to me and furthering the deceit, meant the Insurance Company would take this very serious as the more time we have to spend determining the truth, the greater the severity of the incident. If he lies to me during our recorded interview, it only provides the ultimate evidence I need to show he intentionally misrepresented material facts of the case in order to gain coverage. This was a classic act of fraud that was disrupted by the investigation. Had this case not been investigated, it's possible the deceit could have played itself out.

As you review the case, make note of the manner in which I report my findings and the report format I follow. These reporting formats are my own style and are only included as an example.

CASE II – AUTO REPAIR SCHEME

The Insured, Mr. Randall obtained a quote to have his car repaired then worked with a friendly repair shop that agreed to do the repairs at a significant reduction. When Mr. Randall went to pick up his car and wasn't happy with work, he took it to another shop. The new shop found unrepaired items as well as an inferior paint job. Mr. Randall tried to indicate that damage had been missed by the appraiser and needed more money. The insured had also told the adjuster that the first repair company was paid the entire amount and the Insurance Company's check was signed over to the repair shop. When a copy of the check was ordered by the adjuster it clearly showed it was cashed by the Insured not Performance Detail. When stories don't match, many times an investigator is assigned to look into the matter, thus the reason for the referral. By ordering an investigation, we were able to intervene in this matter before any additional work had been done. The new repair shop saw us in person so knew this claim was being watched.

CASE III – BRAKE CHECKING

In this case we represented the tailgater. The woman driver indicated that she had to brake for a child on a bike but the witness stated this was untrue. The concept of Assault by Brake Checking is a new phenomenon but her actions contributed to this accident and we panned on playing the "criminal charge card" if this matter got out of hand with her personal injury attorney. The attorney got wind of our plans and ended up dropping his client feeling the fight and time wasn't worth the effort. It was our field investigation that led to the discovery of the witnesses which turned this case around dramatically.

CASE IV – SLIP ANF FALL

Ms. Harkow stated that she got up in the middle of the night and went to go use the bathroom only to slip and fall on what she stated was water on the floor. Upon investigating the incident, I learned from the maintenance supervisor that there had been no reported water leaks in the room and no maintenance records of any water related repair. I inspected the room to try and see what she may have tripped on. I looked for a broken or uneven tile, loose carpeting or perhaps an uneven threshold at the bathroom door, but none existed. I learned a security officer was the first responded and I tracked him down at another job he held. Upon taking his statement, he indicated that the woman seemed to have just showered and had a wet head. He believed she had just gotten home and showered. At the same time though he stated that she was had slurred speech and moved slowly and recalled seeing prescription bottles on the night stand. He also recalled the subject stating that she just passed out. From the investigation, this was clearly not a slip and fall where the hotel neglected some hazard that caused the accident. Ruling out the hotel being at fault and documenting all the facts while they were still fresh in everyone's mind was a precautionary measure against any future law suit. I later learned that the woman's father called and wanted a full reimbursement of the woman's two week stay until he was presented with the facts from our investigation at which time he dropped all demands.

CASE V – STAGED PEDESTRICAN ACCIDENT

Mr. Brooke thought he would hang out at a local Feed store until he found an unsuspecting victim. When 75 years old Mr. Rogers exited, Mr. Brooke knew he had found the perfect target. Right as Mr. Rogers started to back out, Mr. Brooke made a bee line directly to the rear of Mr. Rogers's car and acted as if he had been struck by the backing vehicle. The only factor Mr. Brooke over looked was an outdoor security camera that captured everything. It would have been an easier case had we been able to get that video or at least a copy from the local police department. Once learning the video was not an option, securing a statement from the manager that had seen the video was the next best piece of evidence to use to fight the demand. Upon contacting Mr. Brooke's attorney and advising him what we had he dropped Mr. Brooke as a client. As the case continued we attempted to reach Mr. Brooke but he refused to meet.

CASE VI – APARTMENT FIRE

The Harbor Apartments had just been bought by a new company when an electrical fire broke out. The new company was in the process of doing everything they could to repair the reputation of the complex as well as make repairs to a complex that prior management had somewhat neglected. Then another fire broke out and the tenant who was a maintenance man immediately stated it must have been another electrical fire. The new owners of the apartment complex needed the fire investigated immediately. The press had already showed video of the fire on the local news and continued the concern that another electrical fire had broken out at the Harbor apartments. To management the publicity, the corporate owners wanted to know everything they could about the fire. Typically in these cases we conduct what is referred to as a parallel investigation speaking to whomever we can and at the same time trying to stay in touch with the fire department to determine what they know. During a conversation with a fire department officer, I learned the fire was not electrical and started on the porch of the second floor property. I spoke to the manager of the complex who reported that the tenant was a smoker. I interviewed the tenant who reported that he doesn't smoke on the porch he smokes inside the apartment. He however stated that his girlfriend's son, smoke small cigars and since they smell so strongly, he is not allowed to smoke them in the house and usually smokes on the porch. IT was also determined that the son had been smoking a "cigarillo" on the porch balcony 30 minutes before the fire. In the fire departments estimation, this coincided with the start time of the fire.

CASE VII – SECURITY SHOOTING

The apartment complex had just opened and within two weeks' time there was already a shooting on the property. The apartment complex' corporate owners didn't know what to expect next. Would they be sued by the victim? Could their entire investment suddenly be at risk? How did the perpetrator penetrate the gated complex? All of these questions would be answered as the person shot was the security guard who had just arrived for his shift. As soon as he got there he was approached by a subject whom he thought had a question but it turns out he wanted more than just information. The subject grabbed the security guards gun and shot him in the leg then demanded his car to make his getaway. Since the purpose for a security guard is to thwart off criminals, the guard knew when taking the job that there may be some danger involved in the position. After all he was carrying a gun while doing his job. So, once we determined it was the security guard who was shot and not a tenant, the apartment complex' corporate owners breathed a sigh of relief.

CASE I

CONFIDENTIAL

August 19, 2013

Ms. Sally Adjuster
AUTO NORTH INSURANCE
Post Office Box 11307
Naples, FL 33631

REF: Your Claim No.: 120291
Our File No.: FL-0812-003
Claimant: Vicki Santiago
Claimant: Christian Santiago
SSN: 124-46-3840 (Vicki)
SSN: 067-66-5444 (Christian)
D/L: 07/08/2013

Details of Investigation

Investigator: John Bilyk / Claims Resource Incorporated / (877) 274-2000 / www.claimsresource.cc

Dates of Investigation: Wednesday, August 15, 2013 (12:15 p.m. – 5:47 p.m.); Thursday, August 16, 2013 (5:25 p.m. -6:15 p.m.) & Friday, August 17, 2013 (6:05 p.m. – 7:18 p.m.)

Pertinent Information: On Wednesday, August 15, 2013, I was contacted by SIU Ross to immediately proceed to contact the claimant's attorney and request permission to talk to the unrepresented, minor driver. Since the minor driver was reportedly living with her mother the claimant Vicki Santiago, I needed to secure Ms. Santiago's approval prior to speaking with her daughter.

Attorney Contact
Farrow & Rogers- 407.836.2560   Wednesday, August 15, 2012

I learned that the attorney on the file Neal Ricardo had this case in his Kissimmee office and it was being handled by the Attorney's assistant "Lucy". I reached Lucys extension and advised I was heading out to the claimant's residence to speak with the unrepresented minor child, Victoria Ramero who was driving our insured's vehicle. I advised that should there be an issue with this contact to call me immediately on my cell phone number. I also advised I would like to also secure the recorded statement of their two clients, Vicki Santiago and Christian "Santiago" Ramero.

SIU Contact

I contacted the SIU and asked if it was okay if I also did a neighborhood canvass while I was in the area. It was discussed that while in the neighborhood, I should have a picture of a silver 2000 Mazda Protégé to show to the neighbors in determining if perhaps the car was left (garaged) at this residence as opposed to Tampa with insured.

Internet Picture - 2000 Mazda Protégé

A generic looking color picture of a silver 2000 Mazda Protégé was downloaded and printed prior to leaving for the neighborhood inquiry.

Personal Visit - Ms. Victoria Ramero
2528 Dome Ridge Court Kissimmee, FL 34744
3:15 p.m. - 5:22 p.m.

Initially the address was provided as 2526 Dome Ridge and once finding this address was not correct, I returned to my office to run a database address search. The address search showed that the correct address was 2528 Dome Ridge Court. The address search however also showed that two other addresses, seemingly more recent, had also been used since the claimant reported the Dome Ridge Court address. These other two addresses were PO BOX 41162, Kissimmee, FL 34742 and 1043 Metro Resorts Place, Kissimmee, FL 34744.

5:47 p.m.

Nonetheless I returned to the same neighborhood and conducted my inquiries of the resident at 2528 Dome Court as well as the surrounding neighbors. I found the current occupant in 2528 has been there less than one month. A vehicle in the driveway had Texas plates #DB2BI81. The resident in 2526 stated that before the current resident in 2528, there was an American couple at the house and before that a Spanish family occupied the residence. He described the Spanish family comprised of the claimant Vicki Santiago who he identified only as a woman in her late 50's early 60's, a male believed to be Christian and a young female, possibly Victoria. I then showed him the picture of the silver 2000 Mazda Protégé and he stated that he had never seen that vehicle at the residence. He did state that he recalled seeing a green Dodge Caravan and possible a white Honda Civic. He believed the young male person worked at "Lockers" as he wore a shirt with the company's logo.

1047 Metro Resorts Place
Kissimmee, FL 34744   Thursday, August 16, 2012
5:25 p.m.

I proceeded to the claimant's newer address located in a vacation resort now being converted to long term apartment rentals. The community is gated however I was eventually permitted access inside. Upon proceeding to the claimant's residence, no one was home. I waited in the area a short while but after finding they had still not returned home, I exited the area.

1047 Metro Resorts Place
Kissimmee, FL 34744   Friday, August 17, 2012
6:05 p.m. -7:18 p.m.

Once again I returned to the claimant's neighborhood, this time finding both the claimant Vicki and Christian present at the apartment. I introduced myself as a representative of AUTO NORTH, her ex-husband's insurance company. I advised both of them I needed to speak to Victoria Ramero who was reportedly in the pool at the time. Christian left to go get her and while remaining waiting, Ms. Santiago pointed out a large scare on her forehead. I didn't want to give her the impression I didn't care so I took a picture of the scar. I did remind them that they were both represented and that I called their attorney to advise him of this contact. Neither subject had been contacted by their attorney on how to proceed, but I advised that we should not discuss the matter. I reconfirmed though that young Ms. Victoria Ramero was not represented although they stated she was seeking some treatment. I did not discuss the case with either of them but did take the opportunity to obtain a photograph of Mr. Christian Santiago Ramero as well.

As I waited for Christian to walk to the community pool and retrieve Victoria Ramero, I was advised by Ms. Vicki Santiago that the insured, Mr. Hector F. Ramero was on his way to the house. I didn't know if he lived there or was just visiting. I remained tight lipped until he arrived just moments before Ms. Victoria Ramero.

When Ms. Ramero arrived she was clearly wet and had her bathing suit on. She went to the back of the house changed then returned to the front room. I asked her to wait momentarily while I speak to her father, the insured Mr. Hector Ramero in private.

Interview - Recorded Statement of Insured Hector F. Ramero

We walked outside and I asked Mr. Ramero where he lived. I wanted to get it straight whether the insured was estranged or not from his family. He told me that he did live in Tampa at the address I had on records of 12261 Mill Street #305, Tampa, FL 33626. I next asked him how many cars he currently has insured under his own name and he responded two. I next identified myself as a licensed investigator and showed him my state license. I told him I had come to this location to question the driver of the car 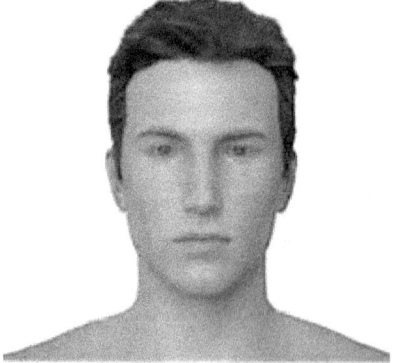 (his teenage daughter) specifically about her possession and use of the car. I told him I had some questions about the story that the car was left while he went to Washington. I could see the anguish in his face and asked if perhaps he just wanted to clear the whole matter up as from this point further it could only get worse if the truth didn't come out. He stated that he bought his daughter the car around June 11, 2013, in Orlando and that the car was given to her. It was meant for her and for her only as his son Christian Ramero already had his own car. Furthermore the car was kept at 1047 Metro Resorts Place, Kissimmee FL 34744-5131 and was never in Tampa or used by him (the insured).

At this point, I advised I would notify the adjuster of this new information and suggested he also call or follow-up after the weekend. He stated that he would like to be able to retrieve his vehicle since he is under the assumption he is not insured. I also walked with him back into the house when he told his ex-wife that she needs to forget trying to get money from his insurance company because he is not insured. I did not render any opinion on what may happen next or how his wife's' attorney may proceed. I think he was just relieved that the truth came out and that no one was seriously hurt.

With the new information coming directly from the insured, I did not proceed with Ms. Victoria Ramero's statement.

Electronic Update   Sunday, August 19, 2013
5:00 p.m.

During this investigation, I maintained contact with the SIU, Shane Ross. Following my completed efforts, I was instructed to submit my full written report for review. The secured recorded statement of Mr. Hector Ramero will be sent directly to the adjuster via US mail.

Status: Closed

Thank you for the continued opportunity to be of service. Should you have any questions regarding this investigation, please contact my office at (877) 274-2000 or direct them to my e-mail.

Enclosure: CD/Recorded statement of Hector F. Ramero sent to Claims Handler via US Mail.

END OF REPORT

CASE II

C O N F I D E N T I A L

January 16, 2013

Mr. Dan Swell REF: Your Claim No. : 124971
NORTH AUTO INSURANCE   Policy No. : N/S
P.O. Box 31114   Our File No. : FL-0113-003
Tampa, FL 3364   Claimant   : Eric Randall
                             SSN   : 250-47-1146
                             D/L   : 10/20/2012

Details of Investigation

Investigator: John Bilyk / Claims Resource Incorporated / (877) 274-2000 / www.claimsresource.cc

Dates of Investigation: Tuesday, January 9, 2013 (3:19 p.m.- 5:25 p.m. & 5:15 p.m.) & Wednesday, January 10, 2013 (10:55 a.m. - 12:33 p.m.)

Pertinent Information: This investigation was received on a rush basis and requested to be initiated immediately. I was advised that the claimant's vehicle was appraised at having $7,860.98 in damages. A check was sent to the claimant for the total of the repair. According to the repair shop, the claimant spent the repair proceeds and couldn't pay the repair shop and wanted to make payments. The claimant agreed to have only certain repairs performed to lower the repair costs. The claimant kept the balance of $7860.98 and the shop actually received a total of $4300.00.

The claimant now alleges that the shop didn't complete work or do all the work needed for repairs. The claimant wants damages that the shop didn't address, which he knew weren't addressed. He has now taken his car to another facility and is requesting more money.

I was requested to visit the Body Shop identified as Performance Detail in Miami and then meet with the claimant to sort out what exactly happened.

Performance Detail 786.944.5582   Tuesday, January 9, 2013

I called the shop and spoke to the owner Mr. Luis Rodriguez. He provided the body shops physical address of 200 SW 46th Avenue Miami, FL 33223. I introduced myself and he agreed to meet with me and attempt to resolve this matter.

Performance Detail -200 SW 46th Avenue Miami, FL 33223

I arrived on site to an unmarked warehouse and small single bay unit and met Mr. Rodriguez. He seemed very straight, but just starting out in business and didn't have much in the way of an office or filing cabinet. Mr. Rodriguez agreed to provide me with a recorded statement.

Recorded Statement of Luis E. Rodriguez DOB 06/27/1986

Mr. Rodriguez while a bit disorganized and newly in business appear to be straight forward and truthful. He advised that the claimant did not sign over any Insurance Company check to him. In fact, the claimant told him he had not coverage and needed to pay for the damage out of his own pocket. Apparently the claimant knows a mutual friend who recommended Luis to him because this body shop is about an hour from the claimant's residence in Boynton Beach.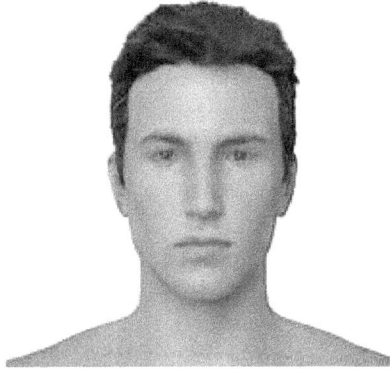
The claimant however reportedly is a welder and works in Miami off Okeechobee Road at Jims Grinding. Mr. Rodriguez stated that the claimant dropped his car off at his shop so he could inspect it and come up with a price to repair the vehicle. Mr. Rodriguez stated he never saw any appraiser's estimate.

After the inspection, Mr. Rodriguez stated that the car needed $1700 for parts and he would charge $2600 in labor. The claimant paid the $1700 in parts which Mr. Rodriguez had no receipt. He then went to Mr. Randall's place of work and picked up an additional $900 in cash. When the car was done, Mr. Randall paid another $1700 final payment for a total repair cost paid to Performance Detail by Mr. Randall of $4300.00. Mr. Randall always paid cash and the only document Luis Rodriguez had of the work is the enclosed work order that doesn't identify the source of the parts, the costs of the parts or even what parts were put on the vehicle. (See attached work order exhibit #1).

Mr. Rodriguez is a young guy and has only been in business for about six months. Mr. Rodriguez feels he was doing a friend of a friend a favor by doing the repairs as inexpensively as possible since he was told there was no insurance money.

When the car was completed, the appraiser came to his shop and inspected the finished vehicle and notice the front left steering arm needed to be replaced. This is when the shop was sent a payment directly to replace the arm. Mr. Rodriguez states he replaced this item and had the receipt for the part (enclosure #2).

While by no means does Mr. Rodriguez appear to have a top rated body shop, the facts about the money between him and the claimant appeared truthful. (Mr. Rodriguez' full recorded statement is enclosed).

Telephone Call Eric Randall - 565.222.3664
5:33 p.m.

I contacted the Randall household in the evening since he was working and thought that perhaps we could meet in the evening. I reached his wife who stated that the claimant works the second shift and doesn't get off until 2:00 a.m. She provided me with his cellular number of 544.955.7668 so I could contact him and discuss meeting. I called him on his cellular phone and left a message. He called me back and we discussed meeting the following day at 11:00 a.m. at his residence.

Electronic Update -SIU Mr. Ross Smith
5:56 p.m.

Immediately following my conversation with Mr. Rodriguez an update was provided to the SIU. We also discussed a request to have a copy of the front and back of the Insurance Company Check paid to the claimant which Mr. Ross forwarded to our office. The claimant had stated that the entire proceeds where paid to Performance Detail.

Personal Visit- Claimant's Residence- 12204 Redlake Drive
Boynton Beach, FL 33426   Wednesday, January 10, 2013
10:55 a.m.

The claimant resides in a secured gated apartment complex where he rents. Mr. Randall met me outside in the parking lot area. His wife later joined us to listen in on the conversation. Mr. Randall agreed to provide me with a recorded statement.

Recorded Statement Eric Randall DOB 5/12/1974 SSN 266-33-1886

Mr. Randall confirmed that the Insurance Company sent him $7860.98 paid directly to him and he used $4300.00 of the funds to pay Performance Detail. He used another thousand to buy tires and rims. He used the remainder to pay his rent as he had lost his job and was facing eviction. He stated that he understands that the rest of the costs are on him and not the responsibly of the carrier. He acted as if he didn't know why I was present and stated that he doesn't want to get involved in any "fraud". Contrary to what I had been told in the initial assignment, Mr. Randall made no attempt to hide the fact that he cashed the check. In fact the check shows the casher's Florida DL

#R333-345-74-042-0. This is the same number that I observed on his driver's license when I asked him for identification. His signature is also on the back of the check. Mr. Randall confirmed he chose Performance Detail because they had a mutual friend. He also paid much less than he was given so he understands that now if he expects to get any further work out of Pro-Detail he will have to resolve this on his own. At the same time the claimant told me his car was located at X-Quisite Auto, located at 1230 W. Lantana Road, Boynton Beach, FL. This is about 15 minutes from the claimant's house and he wanted me to come visit the location. He stated that putting everything aside that there appeared to be one item that the car still needed that the appraiser never saw. This was a right knuckle. I agreed to accompany him to X-Quisite Auto. The claimant's full statement is enclosed).

X-Quisite Auto - 1230 W. Lantana Road, Boynton Beach
12:01 p.m.

Here I met the owner and learned that he and the claimant had been talking to Mr. Shiner of North AUTO INSURANCE to cover the cost of just the right knuckle paid directly to the business. I also was shown about $1,000 worth of work that needed to be performed and was on the original appraisal but not performed by Performance Detail. The shop also stated that the paint job was done in a contaminated booth and had specs of air and particles in the paint. This however again was a matter that needed to be handled between the claimant and Luis Rodriguez. It seemed very clear when I left that the claimant agreed to take care of all other matters and that the payment for the right knuckle would end any further claims.

Electronic Update   Wednesday, January 16, 2013
10:15 p.m.

During this investigation, I maintained contact with the SIU, Mr. Ross. Upon completion of this investigation, I forwarded my full written report for his review.

Status: Closed

Thank you for the continued opportunity to be of service. Should you have any questions regarding this investigation, please contact my office at (877) 274-2000 or direct them to my e-mail.

Enclosure: #1 Performance Detail "Work Order"
#2 Steering Arm Part Replacement Receipt
#3 CD / Statements of Rodriguez and Mr. Randall

END OF REPORT

CASE III

C O N F I D E N T I A L

May 28, 2013

Mr. Mark Woods   REF: Claim No: 132568
NORTH INSURANCE   Our File No : FL-0513-004
Post Office Box 3336   Insured: John Murray
Margate, FL 33374   Claimant: Trina Ann McCormichale
                              SSN : 509-94-0674
                              D/L : 04/01/2013

Details of Investigation

Investigator: John Bilyk / Claims Resource Incorporated / (877) 274-2000 / www.claimsresource.cc

Dates of Investigation: Thursday, April 18, 2013 (12:34 p.m.); Monday, April 22, 2013 (1:13 p.m.); Friday April 26, 2013 (12:54 p.m.- 1:33 p.m.); Monday, May 13, 2013 (1:56 p.m.); May 14, 2013 (3:33 p.m.); Wednesday, May 22, 2013 (11:03 a.m.- 3:31 p.m. & 6:33 p.m.)& Thursday, May 23, 2013 (9:33 a.m.- 2:11 p.m. & 5:30 p.m. - 7:00 p.m.)

Pertinent Information: On Thursday, April 18, 2013, I was advised by SIU, Ross Smith to conduct an accident scene investigation by securing statements from the claimant and any witnesses I could identify. Mr. Smith forwarded me the Police Report purchased from Buycrash.com as well as the claims file notes, insured's information and recorded statement. I reviewed all documentation before proceeding with this investigation.

Telephone Contact -Claimant Trina Ann McCormichale
<u>Telephone Number 352.989.0959   Monday, April 22, 2013
1:13 p.m.</u>

I called the claimant and found she answered the phone during the middle of the day. I advised that the purpose of my call was to inquire as to who represented her. She stated that she did not know the specific attorney however they were with Rogers & Rogers. I did not discuss the case or make any further inquiries and thanked her for her assistance.

<u>Law Offices of Rogers & Rogers 352.552.4459 Friday, April 26, 2013
12:54 p.m.-1:33 p.m.</u>

I contacted the Law Offices and was advised that Attorney Rogers' assistant Michelle Antia was handling this matter. I was advised to send a letter to her attention at mantia@rogersandrogers.com. I compiled the letter and sent it via email to her attention.

Law Offices of Rogers & Rogers 351.542.4459   Monday, May 13, 2013
1:56 p.m.

I called the law offices and again was put through to Ms. Antia's voicemail. I left a detained message asking to take her clients statement and asked if she received my letter.

Law Offices of Rogers & Rogers 351.542.4459   Tuesday, May 14, 2013
3:33 p.m.

I spoke to Attorney's assistant yesterday and she stated that she never received my letter? I resent the same letter to her attention but emphasized that I wanted to secure her clients statement.

Ms. Antia 351.542.4459   Wednesday, May 22, 2013
11:03 a.m.

I sent an email to Attorney Rogers attention reporting that I wasn't sure if they still represented Ms. McCormichale. I advised that I had made numerous attempts to speak with Ms. Antia whom I was directed to no avail. Ms. Antia returned my call, but I was apparently on the other line. She left the most bizarre message stating that she never received any letter from me and has no idea what I am calling about. I immediately called her back and left her a message stating exactly what my intentions were. I also immediately sent her an email making the same request to secure her clients statement. To date I have received no response.

SIU Contact
12:40 p.m.

After this last message, I got the impression they were just stalling because it just didn't make any sense. I also advised the SIU, Mr. Shane Ross that I was still proceeding with the investigation.

Leesburg Police Department 352.787.2121
1:11 p.m.

I reviewed the Police report obtained through BUYCRASH.COM and saw that the investigating officer had put the insured name in the witness box. I had an address but I wanted a name to go along with this information. I spoke to Sonia in records who stated that she would get with Patrolman Secrest and have this information corrected and get back to me.

Telephone Contact Insured- Mr. John Murray
1:31 p.m.

I contacted the Insured and obtained a description the motorcycle as well as the motorcycle operator. The insured advised that the motorcycle was a Harley Davidson black and silver in color and it was driven by a male subject in his 30's tall and thin build with no facial hair. As I was talking to the Insured, he mentioned that the claimant had tried to back her off by hitting her brakes earlier at the intersection of Lone Oak and Main Street. He then stated that she did it again on S. Lone Oak in front of several witnesses who were outside their house at the time. He stated that the claimant stopped for no reason as there were no kids crossing or near the street. Stating "no reason" seemed an incomplete answer so I pushed him more until he stated what he meant was that she stopped to get him off her tail because she felt he was following her too closely. At that point, I realized her actions where what seemed to have caused the accident not the Insured's. I asked if he would allow me to visit him and he reported he was off work on Thursday, so we agreed to meet Thursday at noon-time at his house in Leesburg.

Witnesses Address -20260 Hwy 27 Clermont, FL 34715
2:44 p.m.- 3:12 p.m.

I proceeded to this location and found it was a trailer park called Bee's RV Resort. I spoke to the manager who based on the description didn't know anyone at the park that currently fit that description. I advised that I was working on a name so if she didn't mind I would call her back to see if the name sounds familiar. She state that I could reach her at 352.429.2116.

Leesburg Police Department 352.787.2121
3:31 p.m.

I called Sonia back at Leesburg PD and learned that Officer Secrest would not be on shift until 6:00 p.m. She however stated that she spoke to him and he also had the witness's telephone number. Sonia became skeptical that I even had a copy of the Police Report because she stated that the witness's telephone number was on the report. With the recent law requiring affidavits to secure police report information, Police Departments are very reluctant to help anyone over the phone. I told her we purchased the report through BUYCRASH.COM and that the witness's telephone number was not on the report. She ran her own check and was surprised to see that the witness's telephone numbers are in fact redacted from the HSWV Crash reports from BuyCrash.com. I tried obtain the witnesses telephone number but she just wouldn't do it stating that there may be a legal reason it is withheld. She stated that I would have to talk to the Patrolman or his supervisor at 6:00 p.m. tonight. I left a message for Patrolman

Secrest to call me as soon as he could.

Leesburg Police Department 352.787.2121
6:33 p.m.

I called and spoke to patrolman Secrest's supervisor Sergeant MacDill. He stated that he was going to meet with Patrolman Secrest and have the Police report corrected with the proper name. He however stated that I would have to come to the Police department in the morning to obtain a copy of the full report and submit a sworn statement affidavit per 316.066(3)c. I advised the Sergeant that I would be driving from Kissimmee so please have the report available for pick-up tomorrow.

Leesburg Police Department Leesburg FL   Thursday, May 23, 2013
9:33 a.m.- 10:45 a.m.

I made a personal Visit to the Leesburg Police department and found the report ready for me to pick-up. I secured the Actual Leesburg Police Report which had the witnesses name corrected as well as his telephone number. The witness was identified as John Jacobs with a corresponding telephone number of 561.319.1992.

Bee's RV Resort -352.429.2116
10:55 a.m.

I spoke to the manager again and asked if she knew Mr. John Jacobs. She stated that she did but that he no longer lived in the park. She stated that he lived with his mom and dad and that they left no forwarding address.

Telephone Contact Witness John Jacobs 561.319.1992
11:11 a.m.

I called the witness and received his voicemail. I left a detailed message asking him to call me.

Telephone Contact Insured 352.552.4444
11:20 a.m.

I called the insured and left a message stating that I was in route to his house as arranged.

Insured's Residence 30 Larry Street, Leesburg, FL 34748
11:42 a.m.- 12:44 p.m.

I arrived at the Insured's and observed his crashed Buick parked off to the left of the house in the grass. The Insured stated that the Police have advised that the inoperable car needs to be removed from the front of the property. I proceeded to introduce myself and the Insured agreed to provide a supplemental statement.

Recorded Statement of John Murray DOB 3/27/1984

The claimant reported that the accident occurred around the area of 120 S. Lone Oak drive. He reported that there was a black family outside that saw the whole accident. He also reported that there was another incident where the claimant stopped abruptly. He stated that the claimant was "angry" and while he had backed off from the prior incident she stopped the second time more abruptly. The claimant has a hard time communicating what actually happened but he did state that "she stopped and caused the accident." He stated that she was playing a game and agreed that she stopped on purpose. He didn't think there was anything wrong with her and stated that she walked fast while talking on the phone and spoke to the motorcycle witness and the black family. He stated that her stating there were kids in the street was no true.

After the statement the claimant agreed to show me where the black family lived. We both entered my vehicle and drove about .5 mile from his residence to 120 Lone Oak Drive. I then returned him to his house and thanked him for his assistance.

120 S. Lone Oak Drive, Leesburg, FL 34748
1:10 p.m.-1:27 p.m.

I proceeded to this location and spoke to three people an elderly man, a female in her young late 20's and a male subject in his teens identified as Trevon Been. Mr. Been agreed to provide a statement of what he witnessed.

Statement of Trevon Been DOB 1/12/1994

Mr. Been stated that on the day of the accident he was outside with his two other brothers. Her stated that one of his brothers was on a bike but that they were no were near the road in fact they were on the porch 30 feet away. He stated that he saw the accident happen he saw the claimant hit her brakes a couple of times then slam on the brakes causing the front of her car to dip and the back to raise up high. He stated she even skid her tires stopping so abruptly causing the insured's car to go under her car. He also stated that there were no kids in the street. He stated that "she stopped to see if he would hit her". He stated that the Police came five minutes later and he told them the same story. (Mr. Been's full statement is attached).

Accident Location Surrounding Area
1:33 p.m.

The accident occurred in front of 120 S. Lone Oak Drive. Across the street there is a chain link fence bordering the roadway and a vacant home.

The witness lives to the left and there house is out of view. To the right there is a chain link fence that runs along the street the next house on the right is vacant. These pictures show the image of the street from the insured drivers perspective traveling south on S. Lone Oak Drive.

Telephone Contact Mr. John Jacobs - 561.319.1994
1:42 p.m.

I called Mr. Jacobs again and left a second message.

2:11 p.m.

Mr. Jacobs returned my call and stated that he was at work in Leesburg and not supposed to be on the phone. He advised that he told police everything he had to say and while he was reluctant to get involved he stated that I could call him back at 5:30 p.m. after he got off work.

5:30 p.m.- 6:13 p.m.

I called Mr. Jacobs back and introduced myself. He agreed to provide me with a recorded statement over the phone.

Recorded Statement of John M. Jacobs DOB 1/17/1993

Mr. Jacobs supported the other two statements stating that there were no kids in the road or even near the road. He further confirmed that the nearest people were the black family outside with one teenager on a BMX type bike. He also corroborated the other two statements saying that the claimant stopped for no reason other than to cause an incident. He said she gave no warning and he had to lock up the rear tire of his bike which caused him to go into a slide and almost hit insured. He said he told police and they said oh "she brake checked him". But she didn't just brake check, she slammed on brakes and stopped suddenly. He stated that the claimant was about 18 feet from her and he was about twenty feet from the insured. He stated that he purposely stayed back because she did a similar brake check at the intersection of Main and S. Lone Drive. After the accident he stated that the claimant got out of car and said to motorcycle guy "did you see how close he was following me" and nothing about any kids or children. He also stated that there absolutely were no children in the area and this was not a true statement. He stated he knows this for certain because after almost hitting the insured he rode his motorcycle around both vehicles and there were no kids anywhere. The witness's full statement is attached and he is well spoken and would make an excellent witness.

<u>Internet Law Article</u>
<u>6:15 p.m. – 7:00 p.m.</u>

I did some internet searching and found similar cases across the country and in Florida have been seen as acts of assault where slamming on the brakes was considered "Intent to Frighten".

I have enclosed the following article to better explain this point.

What you may not know is that this tailgate stopping action can lead to both civil and criminal assault charges and can block the front driver from any injury recovery if it actually leads to an accident.

First, let's think about the idea of assault charges. Ask yourself what slamming on the brakes is supposed to accomplish?

The easy answer is to say "to get the other car to back off." But there is an underlying answer that is more important, it is "to scare the other driver into thinking they might rear-end the front car so that they decide to back off." This is the important distinction.

Slamming the brakes is intended to cause fear, fear of a potential accident and possible injury.

The Crime of Assault, in many states, includes any action that is intended to cause fear of immediate harm in the mind of another person.

In Maryland, there is even a specific Criminal Jury Instruction under the category of Assault called "Intent to Frighten." To be found guilty of 2nd Degree Assault in this context, the state must prove 4 things:

That the front car driver committed an act with the intent to place the driver of the second car in fear of immediate physical harm;

That the front car driver had the apparent ability at the time of the action to actually cause physical harm; That the driver of the second car (or any other person in the area) was reasonably put in fear of physical harm; and That the front car driver was not legally justified, or acting in self-defense.

Let's analyze these elements in this context. (1) You intentionally slammed on your brakes, with the intent to scare the second car into thinking if they don't slow down there might be an accident – Check; (2) you are driving a hunk of steel weighing upwards of a ton and if an accident occurs, it is likely to cause at least a minor injury – Check; (3) someone was actually put in reasonable fear that they might immediately be hurt as a result of your action — Maybe; (4) there is no legal justification for slamming on your brakes to scare someone – "he was tail gaiting me" is not a valid justification here.

So, with 3 of the 4 elements being fairly obvious, as long as there is some proof or good faith belief that someone was actually scared as a result of your actions, you just committed an assault.

Florida Police Officer's "Blog" on Slamming on Brakes Topic

I've had this happen to me once. I made the arrest for aggravated assault, the state attorney actually upgraded it to aggravated battery because the person was "jolted" as a result of the accident..........it stuck and the guy pled out......I've heard of other cases, but didn't follow them.

It definitely fits the assault/battery statute here in Florida.....but only an idiot would admit to "slamming on the brakes just so he would hit me".......stupidity he/she deserves to go to jail.....too much road rage and too many idiots causing injuries/death on the roadways.

Electronic Update   Tuesday, May 28, 2013
3:12 p.m.

At this point, it appears there is a case that the claimant slammed on her brakes to scare the claimant and lied about there being children in or near the roadway. Statements from two witnesses, Mr. Bell and Mr. Jacobs confirm what the Insured had a difficult time communicating.

The Law Offices of Rogers and Rogers, specifically Michelle Antia has not assisted or responded to many of our attempts to set an amicable time to interview her client. At this point it seems this case should be submitted to DIF as a Fraud Referral and may also meet the guidelines of criminal assault.

Pending any further developments, I am closing my file in this matter. If future responses are received from the Law Office of Rogers and Rogers I will notify your office to see if we are to proceed.

Case Status: Closed

Should you have any questions regarding this investigation, please contact my office at cases@claimsresource.cc

Enclosures: #1 CD with statements of:
    a. Insured John Murray
    b. Witness Trevon Been
    c. John Jacobs

    #2 Official Leesburg Police Report (5 pages)

END OF REPORT

CASE IV

C O N F I D E N T I A L

December 28, 2012

Ms. Theresa Thomas   REF: Your File No.: 866431
PROPERTY INSURANCE   Our File No. :FL-1212-004
12790 Merit Drive   Addt'l File : N/S
Denver, CO 75251   Subject : Sophia Harkow
                                   D/L : 05/11/2012
                                   SSN   :   473-33-3065
                                   Insured : Paradise Holdings

Details of Investigation

Investigator: John Bilyk / Claims Resource Incorporated / (877) 274-2000 / www.claimsresource.cc

Dates of Investigation: Monday, December 10, 2012 (3:13 p.m.); Monday, December 17, 2012 (12:07 p.m. - 6:15 p.m.) & Tuesday, December 18, 2012 (9:01 a.m.- 4:30 p.m.)

Pertinent Information: Prior to initiating this investigation, I reviewed all information provided by the SIU, Mr. Coates. This information included a detailed description of the accident, the claimant's name and insured contact information.

Doralto Beach Resort - Insured Contact, Ms. Tina Gonzalez
305.797.0065 Extension 3300   Monday, December 10, 2012
3:13 p.m.

The insured's property is called the Doralto Beach Resort. It is a famous Miami Beach Hotel dating back to the 70's when reportedly bands such as the Beatles performed there. I called the hotel and the insured contact Ms. Gonzalez was very pleasant and helpful. I learned the claimant was staying in room #944 at the time of the incident. I also learned that the room is booked through December with some periodic changes in guests specifically on Monday December 17, 2012, after 2:00 p.m. I could gain access to the room and we agreed to meet on that date.

Doralto Hotel 6777 Collins Avenue
Miami Beach, FL
12:07 p.m. - 3:44 p.m.

Monday, December 17, 2012

As agreed, I visited the hotel arriving in the later afternoon after check out and prior to the next guest's check-in time. I was accompanied to the room by Ms. Gonzalez. I examined and photographed the room. The entrance, hall closet and bathroom are all tiled. There were no broken tiles or any uneven surface. There was also no threshold under the bathroom door. As we discussed the way the hotel operated I was advised that the Customer Service Manager manages, maintenance and guest issues. I was advised this person was Mr. Steve Ruiz.

Mr. Steve Ruiz Customer Service Manager

In this hotel, any room repairs, guest complaints or closures of rooms for maintenance are tracked by Mr. Ruiz and the hotels software he uses. He agreed to provide me with a recorded statement.

Recorded Statement of Mr. Steve E. Ruiz

Mr. Ruiz has been working at the hotel for 3.5 years. He stated that room #944 did not have any reported leaks, or problems that could have been associated with the guest's fall. Nor have there been any repairs or changes made to that room since her incident. This subject stated that the day after the fall, he visited with the claimant to see how she was doing and he stated that she seemed to be speaking very slowly. It was a characteristic that stood out to him for such a young and beautiful girl. He described her as a blonde haired 5'5 inch female in her early 20's. He stated that he visited with her the day after the incident. He stated that it is very common for young adults to come to their resort for the club experience. He went onto review her billing portfolio and found she paid for the hotel using an online travel company (Travelocity), but that she paid the add-on Resort Service fee of $15.00 a day for amenities like the gym and beach chairs. He said it is not uncommon for a guest that feels the hotel was responsible for something to ask for a credit of some sort but she paid her full bill when she checked out on May 16, 2012. From the resort Information Invoice (attached) it appears she checked in on May 9, 2012 and checked out on May 16, 2012.

Mr. Ruiz also stated that he reviewed the report prepared by the first responder and since it was 5:50 a.m., that person would have been a security guard. He stated that according to the guard's report, it stated that the guest reported that she "passed out". (Mr. Ruiz' full statement is enclosed)

Security Department

I next visited the Security Office and inquired about the security guard on duty the night of the incident and the report compiled. I obtained a copy of the report (enclosed) which clearly indicated that the claimant stated to the security guard that she "passed out". The security guard on duty that night was a Mr. Mark Paty, badge # 405.

Human Resources

I went back to Human Resource Office where I had first met the insured Contact Ms. Gonzalez. I enquired about the Security Personnel Mr. Mark Paty and learned he was no longer with the

Resort. She pulled his personnel file and I reviewed same. I determined Mr. Paty's personal information to include his SSN 589-50-2308, address 5640 NE Miami Court, Miami, FL phone number 7886.985.8419

Attempted Contact Security Officer/ Witness Mark Paty 786.985.8419
4:45 p.m.

I called and left a message for Mr. Paty. He called me back a few minutes later and stated that he was running errands and that he would not be able to meet today. He stated that possibly tomorrow he would have more time before he went to work at 3:00 pm. I stated I would call him in the morning.

Telephone Contact Mr. Paty
9:11 a.m.

I started to call Mr. Paty early and left several messages. At around 12:00 p.m. I elected to proceed directly to his house.

640 NE Miami Place, Miami, FL
12:53 p.m.- 1:43 p.m.

I arrived at Mr. Paty's house and found no one present. I spoke to several people outside and after several minutes his brother arrived in the area. His brother stated that he had also been trying to reach Mark. He stated that Mark works at the Blue Diamond hotel. I searched the internet and found The Blue Diamond Condominium Resort located at 7115 Collins Avenue, Miami Beach.

Blue Diamond Condominiums
2:22 p.m. - 2:41 p.m.

I proceeded to this location and found these were condominiums and while Mr. Paty was reported to work here he was not scheduled to work this day.

2:55 p.m.

As I was just leaving the area, Mr. Paty called me and stated that his phone's battery had gone dead and he had just arrived at work and was charging his phone when he heard my messages. He stated that he was at another place he works identified as 0801 Brickell Key Boulevard in downtown Miami. He advised that the building was a private high-rise condominium structure and he was working the front security desk. I advised that I needed to come to his location and meet him and he obliged.

Statement of Mark Paty
<u>8801 Brickell Key Boulevard, Miami, FL</u>
<u>3:27 p.m.</u>

I proceeded into downtown area of Miami off Brickell Avenue and the inter-coastal waterway. Mr. Paty was working in an upscale high-rise condominium complex as the front desk attendant. Mr. Paty confirmed that he recalled hearing Ms. Harkow state that she does not remember what happened as she passed out. He also stated that she appeared as if she had just got home and he believed her hair was wet as if she had also just showered. He also remembered her talking slow and saw what appeared to be prescription medicine bottles on her night stand. She did not smell of alcohol, but appeared as if she had been up and had just come home and showered. She may have been under the influence of something but he didn't think alcohol. He stated he was certain that she did just wake up to use the bathroom.

<u>SIU Electronic Update   Friday, December 28, 2012</u>

Following the completion of these efforts, I forwarded my final report to the SIU, Mike Mathews.

Case Status: Closed

Should you have any questions regarding this investigation, please contact my office at cases@claimsresource.cc

Enclosures: #1 – CD statements of Mr. Ruiz and Mr. Paty
                #2 – Copy of Security Incident Report
                #3 – Copy of Information Invoice (check-out)

END OF REPORT

CASE V

C O N F I D E N T I A L

January 16, 2014

Ms. Pamela King	REF: Your File No.: 143301
INSURANCE COMPANY	Our File No. : FL-0114-007
Post Office Box 33444	Addt'l File : N/S
Miami, FL 3334	Insured : Jerry Brooke
	Claimant : Eddy Rogers
	D/L : 11/14/2013
	SSN : 116-68-0953

Details of Investigation

Investigator: John Bilyk / Claims Resource Incorporated / (877) 274-2000 / www.claimsresource.cc

Dates of Investigation: Monday, January 6, 2014 (10:19 a.m.); Wednesday, January 8, 2014 (11:50 a.m.- 12:55 p.m.); Friday, January 10, 2014 (9:55 a.m., 2:23 p.m. & 3:35 p.m.); Monday, January, 13, 2014 (1:11 p.m.-1:44 p.m.)& Tuesday, January 14, 2014 (12:05 p.m.- 4:36 p.m.)

Pertinent Information: On Monday, January 6, 2014, I was requested to follow-up and attempt to secure or view security video footage currently in the custody of the Miami Police Department or attempt to locate another copy from the originating business Sheila's Feed & Garden Supply. This security video from Sheila's Feed & Supply reportedly captured the actual incident in which the claimant claims he was struck by the Insured.

Investigation   Wednesday, January 8, 2014
11:50 a.m.

I reviewed the assignment, the police report and a report prepared by an Independent Adjuster. The Police report # 13-737611 indicated that the responding Officer was J. A. Trecker, Badge # 44841. Officer Trecker states in the narrative that "PED 1 failed to make any attempt to move out of harm's way and continued to walk into the back of VEH 1". The officer clearly seems to indicate that this matter was avoidable by the pedestrian. As such, the SIU wanted to also evaluate the video having more extensive experience with staged accidents or deliberately planned accidents. I spoke to the IA as requested and found they could not corroborate the Officers narrative statement and had not secured a copy of the security video.

Police Department - 305.931.6500
12:12 p.m. - 12:20 p.m.

I learned that Officer Julie Trecker had advised that her copy of the video had been turned into evidence and she no longer had access to the video. Her immediate division supervisor was identified as Sergeant Figuerero. Both he and Officer Trecker work the 6:30 a.m. - 5:25 p.m. shift. I left a detailed message for Sergeant Figuerero asking him to contact me.

Wonders & Flankers Attorney at Law - 305.226.9700
12:55 p.m.

I called the Law Offices of Wonders & Flankers and asked to speak with Attorney Marc E. Wonders, the Attorney on the letter of representation sent to INSURANCE COMPANY. I was advised that Michelle was the case manager on the file but them was put with Ms. Susie Mathews who stated that she was handling the file. She indicated that arranging a recorded statement was fine with the Attorney but that they have had some difficulty contacting their client. She indicated that his phone is a "Magic-Jack" internet phone that makes reaching him a challenge. She stated that he usually treats once a week and would leave a message with the doctor for him to call the office so that an amicable time could be arranged for the statement. I provided Ms. Mattos with my direct contact number.

Miami Police Department - 305.931.6500
Follow-up   Friday, January 10, 2014
9:55 a.m. & 2:23 p.m.

I again called the Miami Police Department and spoke to the Captain, who stated that he would speak with Sergeant Figuerero. I called back again and was told that Sergeant Figuerero advised that the video would not be release but he did not comment about whether I could come in and personally view it myself. I left another message asking for a response to this request.

Telephone Contact DIF - Field Office
Investigator Captain Michaels 305.972.8622
3:35 p.m.

I spoke to the Investigator Michaels and asked if he had any suggestions on having the opportunity to get a copy of the security video at least have the opportunity to watch it at the Miami PD. He stated that he could lend no assistance but that upon completion of our investigation to forward the matter as quickly as possible and they would review the file and video.

Sheila's Feed & Garden Supply
Telephone Contact 305.932.9775   Monday, January 13, 2014
1:11 p.m. - 1:44 p.m.

I contacted the feed store and spoke to Mr. Gonzalez, the store Manager. He stated that the assistant Manager Fred Jacob handled the entire incident with the patron/insured, the police and the claimant. He stated that after the incident, he met with the police and made them a copy of the incident. As per their store policy, a second copy of the video was made and sent to the owner who has still not be able to locate the second copy. Having heard that Mr. Jacob watched the video and made the copies, Mr. Gonzalez agreed to allow me to secure a recorded statement from Mr. Jacob. We agreed to Tuesday, January 14, 2014, at 2:00 p.m.

Sheila's Feed & Garden Supply , Inc. 513 South Avenue
Miami, FL 33612   Tuesday, January 14, 2014
12:05 p.m. - 4:36 p.m.

As I arrived I observed the stores exterior camera located to the left of the front door covering anyone coming in and out of the front door. The business is located directly on Nebraska Avenue which has a high flow of traffic. Directly across the street to the north perpendicular to South Avenue is a low income apparent complex. It does not appear to be unusual for people from this complex or the side street to walk through the Feed Stores parking lot which is located on the corner. The positioning of the camera not only covers the front door but also the 4-5 spaces in front of the door and those headed towards Nebraska. I again met with Mr. Gonzalez who stated that the owner was on vacation until Saturday, January 18, 2014, so that he could not follow-up with him concerning the video copy he might have or was looking for. We agreed to touch base on this matter the week of January 20th after the Owner returns home. Meanwhile he introduced me to his assistant manager who took me in the office where the security camera monitor is located. From the office I observed the actual angle of the cameras and the area of coverage depicted in this position.

The top image is from the actual security camera and the Insured, Mr. Brooke was believed to be parked in the space where you currently see the silver compact. The next car over almost out of screen is a dark SUV and that direction is west towards Nebraska Avenue.

After speaking briefly, I learned there were no other potential witnesses and that Mr. Jacob handled the entire incident from responding to the initial incident, speaking with the claimant, reviewing the video and copying the footage for the Police. He agreed to provide a recorded statement.

Recorded Statement Fred Jacob DOB 1/2/1979

Mr. Jacob has been working at the feed store for 3 years. On the date of the incident, he stated that he had recalled seeing the claimant and two other individuals hanging around outside the exterior of the business. This activity in itself is not unusual because people in this area sometimes come up close to the business to get out of the sun or to learn against the building and just hang out or wait for someone. He stated that the Insured, Mr. Brooke is a regular customer but that the claimant was not known nor was he a customer on this day. He described the claimant as a darker skinned male wearing a du-rag.

He stated that the car was already in motion when the claimant came into the security camera picture and walked into the back of the car. He stated that it looked faked in his opinion. The other two people he was with, a woman and a child, they were not with him but stayed behind and after the incident occurred those to other people didn't react surprised about the incident. They just walked over and didn't seem overly concerned or worried like you would expect after someone you know is hit by a car. The witness stated that having seen the video and during his interaction with the claimant he just didn't believe he was injured. After the incident, the Insured left because he felt threatened by the claimant. While the insured left and called the police, he later returned. The claimant remained at that location the entire time and stood outside yelling and causing a major disturbance. He was swinging his arms and walking around. Just by his movements, he didn't seem to be injured at all. When the police returned so did the fire department and an ambulance. The claimant left via the ambulance (the entire recorded statement in two parts is attached).

SIU Contact

Following this interview, I contacted the SIU and discussed the matter. I advised that I was still waiting on the opportunity to secure the claimant's statement, however based on the witness and the police officer's comments; both felt the incident was staged. Therefore, I was instructed to prepare this interim report for the SIU to facilitate a quicker referral to DIF.

Electronic Update   Thursday, January 16, 2014

During the course of this investigation I maintained contact with the SIU, Ms. Jenny Davis.

At this time, I am forwarding this interim report and will continue to pursue the claimant's statement through his attorney.

Case Status: Open, pending claimant's statement.

Enclosure: #1 -CD Recorded statements from witness Fred Jacob

Should you have any questions regarding this investigation, please contact my office at cases@claimsresource.cc

END OF REPORT

CASE VI

C O N F I D E N T I A L

May 16, 2013

Ms. Rosemary Brooks   REF: Your File No.: 05-303
NORTH INSURANCE   Our File No. :FL-0513-003
233 Meadowlands Parkway   Addt'l File : N/S
Secaucus, NJ 07094   Claimant : None
                                  D/L :   4/24/2013
                                  Insured: Venetian Group Inc.

Details of Investigation

Investigator: John Bilyk / Claims Resource Incorporated / (877) 274-2000 / www.claimsresource.cc

Dates of Investigation: Wednesday, May 8, 2013 (9:02 a.m.); Thursday, May 9, 2013 (3:39 p.m. -6:00 p.m.) & Monday, May 13, 2013 (9:59 a.m.- 2:12 p.m. & 4:17 p.m. -5:01 p.m.)

Pertinent Information: On Wednesday, May 8, 2013, I was contacted by the SIU, Mr. Sam Gates and requested to secure the statements of the Property Manager and any person identifiable as responsible for the fire. I was also requested to secure a copy of the Fire Marshals and tenants lease where the fire occurred.

The SIU provided me with contact information for my insured contact on the property, Ms. Christine West.

Telephone Contact - Harbor Walk Apartments Property Manager
Ms. Christine West 813.884.1821   Thursday, May 9, 2013
3:39 p.m.-4:44 p.m.

I spoke to Ms. West over the phone and she requested that I put together what I needed in writing and send it to her attention. I prepared an email and sent it to her email address at

Christine_West@venetian.net. We then agreed to meet on Monday at 11:00 a.m.

Early New Articles Review
6:00 p.m.

Early news articles clearly raised the concern that this may have been an electrical fire. There was an electrical fire in February 2013, which was referred to as an electrical short but I would later hear from the Property manager that this was attributed to too many items plugged into a power strip. The news fueled this concern that the new fire may also be electrical in nature. This was an early report by the Tampa ABC Action News. http://www.abcactionnews.com/dpp/news/harbour-walk-fire-ignites-resident-fears.

The local channel 10 did the same story raising concerns that the fires may be linked to electrical problems at the complex but according to Hillsborough County Code Enforcement there had been no violations and it was too early to speculate if this was also electrical in nature.

http://www.wsls.com/story/22065586/3-alarm-apartment-fire-in-west-tampa

Personal Visit- Harbor Walk Apartments - 8302 Crystal Harbor Drive Tampa, FL 33615   Monday, May 13, 2013
9:59 a.m.- 2:12 p.m.

I made a personal visit to the Harbor Walk Apartments and met with Ms. Christine West. After speaking momentarily, she agreed to provide a recorded statement.

Recorded Statement Ms. Christine J. West DOB 11/6/1969

Ms. West advised that she was present on the day of the fire. She has worked regular shifts since the fire and has not been advised or contacted by anyone concerning any injuries or vehicle damage. She stated that the fire was initially spotted at the unit of their landscape worker, Ricardo Gonzalez. It was around 11:30 a.m. when the fire started and the worker, his girlfriend and her son where all in the apartment at the time. They had plenty of time to get out of the building and also make certain everyone else was evacuated. Most tenants were at work at the time. Ms. West provided me the most recent rental agreement for Mr. Gonzalez, which has a work4rent agreement (attached 5 pages). Mr. Gonzalez is provided an apartment valued at $595.00 a month in return for 20 hours a week. Ms. West had also just received the Fire Marshall's Cause and Origin report which stated the fire occurred on the balcony and the cause of the fire was a pipe or cigar. Ms. West had asked if this included cigarettes since the employee Ricardo Gonzalez smoked. The fire investigator said yes, and added that the young man in the apartment admitted to the investigators that he was smoking on the porch about a half hour earlier which seemed to coincide with the time the fire started. I obtained a copy of the fire marshals report. (Ms. West' full statement has been enclosed)

I next met and introduced myself to the landscaper and tenant who receives his rent for free under the apartments Work4Renk agreement. He agreed to sit down and provide me with a recorded statement.

Ricardo Perez DOB 3/24/1975 SSN 582-27-2967

I asked Mr. Gonzalez if he had any form of renters insurance but he did not. He started out telling me he didn't smoke or at least not out in public where anyone could see that he smoked, but I told him Ms. West has seen him many times smoking on property. He then stated that he smokes inside his house and has no reason to smoke on the porch. He tried to state that the fire was most likely from the light switch outlet but I advised that the fire and arson investigators determined that it was from a smoking device. He stated that no one was smoking on the porch, but I told him his girlfriend's son stated to fire investigators that he had just smoked on the porch. He then said that he was in the room with his girlfriend who was still sleeping, so maybe the boy went out on the balcony unbeknownst to him. I told him the cause of the fire appears to be a pipe or cigar and asked if the boy smoked a pipe. He thought I meant crack or pot so I asked does he smoke either and he said no. He said he smokes those "cigarillos" (which the kids call blunts). They are flavored thin cigars and he stated that he purchases them at the local convenience store. He stated that he doesn't let the boy smoke them in the house because he doesn't like the smell. He stated that his girlfriend is not on the lease as she wasn't staying with him full time but was there a lot. Then her son also moved in with them but he didn't want to inherit the whole family so he told her the boy could not stay and she has since moved out. The employee stated that they had a lot of time to make sure everyone got out of the apartments and most were empty with the exception of the "old man" downstairs, whom they alerted and got out. He stated that no one was hurt and no cars were damaged in the fire.

The employee told Ms. West that he was working at the time as he should have been doing. But he stated in this statement and the statement to the fire investigators that he was inside when the fire started. It appears that while he was supposed to be working he was still in the apartment. The claimant stated that his girlfriend's name was "Angelique Vasquez" and her son's whom he knew as "Danny Dominguez". He stated he didn't know their birth dates.

The employee holds no other full or part time job. He does do some graphic design work from home but has not formal employer. His girlfriend reportedly works for a telemarketing company, her son's employment is not known. (The employee's full statement is enclosed)

National Database - Address Cross Reference and Name Searches
4:17 p.m. - 5:01 p.m.

I referred to a national database to do an address search and cross reference possible names matches for the girlfriend and her son. I identified the claimant's girlfriend as Angelique Katherine Vasquez DOB 11/14/1974 (38) SSN 073-53-9343 and her son Benito "Danny" Dominguez DOB 2/4/1994 (21) no verifiable SSN.

SIU Electronic Update   Wednesday, May 15, 2013

During the course of this investigation, I maintained contact with the SIU. As it turns out the Fire Marshals report just released May 9, 2013 states that the "area of origin" for the fire was the exterior balcony and that the "heat source" was a pipe or cigar. This puts to rest any speculation the fire was electrical or in any way related to the fire in February 2013. Furthermore the employee/tenant stated that his girlfriend's son smoked cigars and according to the fire investigators he had been smoking a half hour earlier on the balcony around the estimated time the fire started. Fortunately, there were no injuries or vehicles damaged.

Pending, review of this matter and any further follow-up request, I will close my file.

Case Status: Closed

Should you have any questions regarding this investigation, please contact my office at cases@claimsresource.cc

Enclosures: #1 Tenant Lease -Ricardo Gonzalez (5 pages)
                #2 Fire Report (6 pages)
                #3 CD with statements of:
                      a. Property Manager Christine West
                      b. Tenant/Employee Ricardo Perez

END OF REPORT

CASE VII

C O N F I D E N T I A L

November 2, 2012

Ms. Rhonda Blank	REF: Your File No. : 04-315
CLAIMS MGMT	Our File No. : FL-1112-001
33A Jefferson Parkway	Addt'l File : N/S
Atlantic City, NJ 07094	Insured : RS MGMT, LLC
	D/L : 09/19/2012

Details of Investigation

Investigator: John Bilyk, CFE / Claims Resource Incorporated / (877) 274-2000 / www.claimsresource.cc

Dates of Investigation: Monday, October 22, 2012 (10:10 a.m.); Thursday, October 25, 2010 (1:17 p.m.- 5:30 p.m.) & Thursday, November 1, 2012 (3:55 p.m. - 7:57 p.m.)

Pertinent Information: Prior to initiating this investigation, I reviewed all information provided by the SIU, Mr. Coates. This information included a detailed description of the accident and a copy of the incident report from the on-site property manager.

Telephone Call Insured Contact
Wendy Riles 854 .249.6714   Monday, October 22, 2012
10:10 a.m.

On the above date I left a message for my Insured Contact Ms. Riles. Her voice mail message stated that she would be back on Thursday October 25, 2012

Return Call Ms. Riles   Thursday, October 25, 2012
12:10 p.m.

I call Ms. Riles who advised that I should call the Regional Manager, Isabelle Mattingly at 954.7797950. I then called Ms.

Mattingly that advised she would call the on-site property manager, Ms. Falls and advise that I was on my way.

Insured Apartment Complex- Sorrento at Sarasota
8991 SW 41st Street, Sarasota, FL 33025
1:17 p.m.

Here I met with Ms. Falls who was actually quite knowledgeable about the incident and therefore I proceeded to take her recorded statement

Recorded Statement Property Manager Ms. Falls

Ms. Falls reported that she received a call from resident Porchia Cinder who lives in Building 4 unit #102. Ms. Cinder's phone number is 727.724,9256. According to Ms. Cinder's file she works at Northwest Farms with a phone number of 727.493.1600. The phone call came in around midnight but Ms. Falls did not hear the message until 5:30 a.m., as she was getting ready for work. Reportedly, the victim was not an unknown party but instead a Security Guard coming to duty. He had just arrived and was on the phone to check in with his office. He was employed by Best Security. At the time of the shooting, several building were still unfinished and the General Contractor/ First Construction hired the guard service to protect the unfinished buildings. At that time the electronic gates were also not working yet or in use, so anyone could come and go unlike today where a security access is required to enter the community.
The guard/victim was identified as a black Haitian male. The attacker was reportedly also a black Haitian man and was being spoken to in Creole. The guard thought it was a joke until he was shot and pulled from his car. It's uncertain if there was a struggle or if the guard was shot with his own gun or the assailants.

According to Ms. Falls, she observed a trail of blood starting on the main entrance road just west of the mailboxes and leading to the sidewalk near the office. There was reportedly another guard on the property, but he was in the back near the unfinished buildings and apparently not around to help. Ms. Falls explained that she tried to identify the Security Officer and called Best Security, but never received a response.
She never had anything to do with the guard service since they were hired by the GC.

After the statement we walked the property and she pointed out where the incident occurred. The picture to the left depicts the entrance to the community. He stopped just past the open gates near the side walk in his car. After being pulled from his car and shot in the leg, he then walked back towards the gates and stopped in the picture to the right in front of the mailboxes building where the blood stops and he was apparently assisted.

Best Security 305.919.9400

After several calls I reached the reported owner Neal Blackshear. He was very reluctant to provide any information. I asked for the guards name and address so I could check up and see how he was doing. He stated that he really don't know much as he was not involved in the incident. It sounded odd that the owner didn't know much about one of his guards getting shot. He deferred me to his HR Manager, Ms. Brown and stated that she would call me back. I asked if he could at least me the name of the guard/victim. He paused and then advised his name was Elliot Winters.

To date the Human Resource Manager has not called me.

Sarasota Police Department, Sarasota Florida
3:55 p.m.-4:20 p.m.

I visited the Sarasota PD and found case #120903902 still an open investigation being conducted by Detective Sam Tort and therefore the report was not available. I called Detective Tort at 727.602.4162 and asked if he could return my call.

Florida Department of Agriculture-Division of Licensing
5:01 p.m.

I checked the States Website for Security Guards and found only one Elliot Winters, with an address in Palm Bay, a Central Florida city.

WINTERS, ELLIOT

License Number Expires   Status
D 13332170   11/17/2013   LICENSE ISSUED

Physical Address
1332 HOLBROOK RD NW
PALM BAY FL 32907

National Comprehensive Database
5:30 p.m.

I ran a national database and found an Elliot Winters DOB 1/20/1983 SSN 0866-76-4617 at 3464 Cluster Road, Sarasota, Florida 33025-4179. I also found another address with an overlapping October date. This address was 1644 NW 24th Place, Madeira Beach, FL 33054.

Continued Investigation Locate Elliot Winters- 3463 Cluster Road, Sarasota, Florida 33025-4179   Thursday, November 1, 2012
3:55 p.m.

I arrived at the above address and found this townhouse apartment occupied by Mr. Jean who also works at Best Security. He and Elliot use to be roommates but since the accident he stated that Elliot's WC check was not enough to maintain his share of the rent so Elliot moved in with some family. He did not know the address, but knew it was on 24th Place. He did however have Elliot's cellular phone number of 954.391.0332.

Elliot Winters - Telephone Contact 727.391.0332
6:12 p.m.

I called the number provided and reached Ms. Winters. He confirmed that his address was 1644 NW 24th Place, Madeira Beach, FL 33054.
He reported he moved back in with some cousin's but was going to look for his own place. I asked if I could come and meet with him and he complied.

Claimant Current Address
1644 NW 24th Place, Madeira Beach, FL 33054
6:36 p.m.- 7:57 p.m.

I arrived at the above address and was greeted at the door by Mr. Winter's younger cousin. He invited me inside and walked me to a bedroom in the back of the house off the back porch. I met Mr. Winters who was lying in bed watching television. He agreed to provide a recorded statement.

Recorded Statement-Elliot Winters DOB 1/27/1983 SSN 084-74-4447

I identified the subject by his state issued Security Guard License. He advised that he used to live in Palm Bay when he first applied for a security guard license. Mr. Winters advised that he had just reported to work and was checking in with the office, when the attack occurred. He stated that Best Security has a special number the guards use to call in to when they arrive onsite for their shift. He was going to relieve another subject that was already present but working in the back. He stated he didn't remember the other guards name but knew he was an African American Male. The subject identified himself as a Haitian male and reported that the male that car jacked him and

shot him in the leg also appeared to be Haitian. The subject reported no ties between him and his attacker. The subject stated that the post is an unarmed post and he is an unarmed guard. When the attacker approached him he said in Creole, "do you speak Creole". He then said put your hands up and the subject put his hands up even though he never saw a gun. He then said give me all your stuff and pulled the subject from the car. The attacker then for no apparent reason shot him once in the lower leg, shin area and the bullet exited from his. The subject never saw the gun, but heard and felt it. He fell to the ground and starting yelling for help. He doesn't quite remember how far he ran but he remembers several people coming out of the buildings and he yelled that guy took my car pointing as the attacker left in the subject's car. The subject then stated that someone had called an ambulance which he left in. He stated that he is on Worker Compensation and initially only received a little over 200 hundred dollars but didn't know it was just a partial check. He just received a check for around $425.00 which seems to be his set biweekly amount. He had never reported his car stolen so I assisted him in calling Guardian Insurance and reporting the stolen vehicle. The subject told me that he had been contacted by Detective Saint Fort and advised that his car had been recovered and is currently being stored at Midtown Towing. The car however is stripped and the subject feels it is totaled.

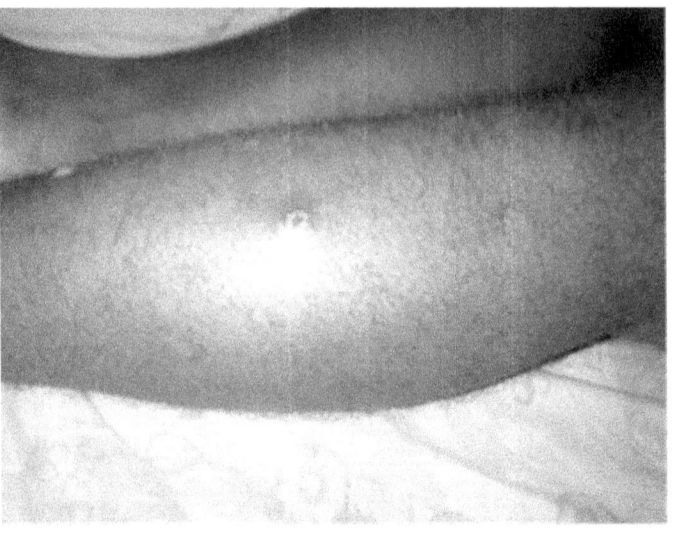

The bullet entered the lower front of the subject left leg and exiting through his calf. His doctor told him it may take a year for him to fully recover as the bullet tore up a lot of nerves leading to his foot and it hurts him to walk without crutches. He was appreciative that RS Management, LLC showed an interest in his condition. (For more information please listen to the recorded statement attached).

<u>Electronic Update</u>   <u>Friday, November 1, 2012</u>

During this investigation I maintained contact with the SIU, Mike Coates. During this time we discussed the fact that the victim was a Security Guard and was there to guard and provide security to the unfinished apartments. As a Security Guard, it appears unlikely any potential claim for lack of security seems to be moot. Secondly, this activity occurred during his scope of employment and as a Security Guard would have understood the dangers involved in his occupation and trained to expect the same. It's unfortunate that he underestimated his attacker as he thought it was a prank since there has never been any problems at the Insured's Property, Sorrento at Sarasota.

Having completed the assignment, the SIU advised me to submit my full written report and send the Claims Handler, Ms. Blank the statements on CD.

Case Status: Closed, pending further authorization to proceed as directed.

Thank you for the continued opportunity to be of service. Should you have any questions regarding this investigation, please contact my office at (877) 274-2000 or via e-mail at cases@claimsresource.cc.

Enclosures : #1 – CD Statements of Ms. Falls and Mr. Winters

End of Report

CHAPTER 9 – RELEASES AND AFFIDAVITS

I. PRINTABLE RELEASES AND AFFIDAVITS

1. Authorization / Release to Interview or Photograph a Minor
2. Medical Release in Spanish
3. No Insurance Affidavit
4. Credit or General Release
5. HIPPA Medical Release

AUTHORIZATION FOR INTERVIEW/PHOTOGRAPHS OF A MINOR CHILD

To whom it may concern:

I hereby authorize/consent _____ and/or it's representative to interview and/or photograph the following individual _____, a minor child.

I_____ do hereby affirm that I am the Parent/Legal Guardian of the above named minor.

THIS IS NOT A RELEASE OF ANY CLAIM I MAY HAVE.

Parent/Guardian _____

Witness _____   Date _____

AUTORIZACION PARA INFORMACION MEDICA

Fecha _____

A Quien le Pueda Interesar:

Yo, _____ autorizo a _____,

o uno de sus representantes, paraque adquieran toda la informacion necesaria acerca de _____ _____, con respecto a alguna enfermedad o accidente, historia medica, consulta medica, tratamiento, rayos x, y copias de los archivos medicos. Una copia de esta autorizaccion es tan efectivo y valido como el original de todos los documentos de hospital.

ESO NO LIBERA ALGUNA DEMANDA QUE YO PUEDA TENER

Testigo _____
(witness)

Firma _____
(signed)

NO-INSURANCE AFFIDAVIT

I, _____ was involved in an accident with

_____

I further state that there are no liability insurance policies in my household for which coverage would apply for this vehicle.

Vehicle Identification No. _____ Year _____ Make _____ Model _____

Signature _____   Date _____

Address: _____

_____

Signed and witnessed this _____ day of _____ 20___.

Special Investigator _____

AUTHORIZATION/RELEASE

I authorize any merchant, credit reporting agency, vendor, financial institution, bank, utility company, telephone company, credit card company, insurer, insurance agent, employer, Internal Revenue Service representative, or other person, to whom a signed or photocopy of this authorization is delivered, to furnish any information, reports or copies of records which may be requested by _____ or their representatives for the purpose of:
_____
_____

This release shall stay effective until the claim is settled.

Date Signed: _____   _____
                                                         Signature of Policyholder

                                                         _____
                                                         Social Security Number

STATE OF _____

COUNTY OF_____

BEFORE ME, the undersigned officer, duly authorized to administer oaths and take acknowledgements, personally appeared _____, to me well known and known to be the person(s) described in and who executed the foregoing Authorization/Release, and he/she/they acknowledged to and before me that he/she/they executed the same freely and voluntarily, and for the uses and purposes therein expressed.

WITNESS my hand and official seal in the County and State last aforesaid this _____ day _____, 20 _____.

                                                              _____
                                                              Notary Public Signature
                                                              State of _____

Stamp / My Commission Expires:

AUTHORIZATION FOR USE AND DISCLOSURE OF PROTECTED HEALTH INFORMATION
UNDER HIPAA RULE 164.508 (Page 1 of 2 Pages)

You May Refuse to Sign This Authorization

I, _____, (hereafter referred to as "Individual") hereby authorize_____, (hereafter collectively referred to as "you") to use and disclose in any form or format a copy of records concerning Individual but only as follows, to: _____for the purpose(s) of (be specific):_____I specifically authorize you to use and disclose the following types of super-confidential information (initial where appropriate):

___ HIV records (including HIV test results) and sexually transmissible diseases
___ Alcohol and substance abuse diagnosis and treatment records
___ Psychotherapy records
___ Tuberculosis
___ All hospital records
___ All of the above

I specifically authorize you to use and disclose the following Protected Health Information. Please initial one or more of the following, if applicable:

Written Medical records
___ X-rays/MRI/CT
___ Billing records
___ Prescription records
Other(specify in detail):

_____
___ All of the above

I understand that my records may be subject to re-disclosure by recipient(s) and unprotected by federal or state law; that this Authorization remains effective until the following date: _____; OR the following event:_____; or until you actually receive a signed revocation or until the records retention period required under federal and Florida law has expired, whichever first occurs; that I have been given an opportunity to ask questions; that I have received a copy of the signed Authorization; that I may inspect a copy of my protected health information to be used or disclosed under this Authorization; that you have not conditioned provision of services to or treatment of me upon receipt of this signed Authorization; and that I may refuse to sign this Authorization. My refusal to sign will not affect my eligibility for benefits or enrollment, payment for or coverage of services, or ability to obtain treatment, except as provided on this form. If the purpose of this Authorization is for the use and/or disclosure of health information for a research study, and I refuse to sign this Authorization, you reserve the right to deny treatment associated with such research. If the purpose of this Authorization is to disclose health information to another party based on health care that is provided solely to obtain such information, and I refuse to sign this Authorization, you reserve the right to deny that health care. I understand that I may inspect or copy the information that is used or disclosed. I understand that I may revoke this Authorization at any time by notifying you in writing, except to the extent that action has been taken in reliance on this Authorization; or if this Authorization is obtained as a condition of obtaining insurance coverage, other law provides the insurer with the right to contest a claim under the policy or the policy itself.

A copy of this signed form will be provided the individual.

By Patient: _____ Date: _____

Or

By Patient's Representative: _____ Date: _____

(Print name, sign, and describe authority below)

_____ _____

_____

(HIPPA MEDICAL RELEASE- Page 2 of 2 pages)

CHAPTER 10 - LEGAL NOTES

STATUTES FOR STATEMENTS

I. Generally, recorded statements including recordings of telephone conversations, when relevant and when properly authenticated, may be admissible in evidence. Southern Mill Creek Products v. Delta Chemical Co., Fla. App. 1967, 203 So.2d 53.

II. Recorded statements, like written statements, can only be used for impeachment purposes. Before the statement can be used, the circumstances of the statement, sufficient to designate the particular occasion, must be mentioned to the witness and he must be asked whether or not he made such statements. Florida Statute 90.101.

See Also: Hancock v. McDonald, Fla. App 1963, 148 So2d 56 where the Appellate Court specifically upheld the ruling of the lower Court in refusing to permit the use of a statement for impeachment purposes where the witness, being impeached, was not given the time, place or circumstances of the alleged contradictory statement.

III. Written transcripts of recorded statements are not admissible when the court reporter who made the transcripts was not present when the recordings were made. Written transcripts violated the "best evidence rule", and, under the circumstances, were pure hearsay. Duggan v. State, Fla. App. 1966, 189 So2d 890.

IV. However, the transcript of a recorded statement may be admissible when the person who personally made the recording publishes the transcript of the tape recording and properly authenticates the recording. Grimes v. State of Florida, Fla. Sup. Ct. 1971, 244 So.2d 130.

V. Florida S.S. 92.33 which requires that any person who takes a written statement from an injured person (personal injury or property damage) shall, at the time of taking such statement, give the witness a copy of the statement, is not applicable to a tape recorded statement of an injured party. The Greyhound Corporation v. Clark, Fla. App. 177, 347 So.2d 732.

Author

John Bilyk has been a career Private Investigator for over 30 years. After graduating from West Chester University of Pennsylvania, he joined a Private Investigative Firm specializing in Insurance Claims Investigations. He has worked his entire career as a Private Investigator learning the Insurance Defense industry. John has been involved in more than 50,000 cases and is considered an Expert in Claims Investigations and Surveillance.

John Bilyk has been using various training material and he recruited and trained his investigative staff. He attained his Certified Fraud Examiner designation, CFE status in 1995. He was licensed and practiced as a Private Investigator in 12 States throughout the U.S. and the Commonwealth of Puerto Rico.

Anyone exploring a career in Private Investigators should take a good look into the Claims Defense Industry. It provides a challenging and consistent flow of work in a professional environment. Whether as a contracted Investigator through an Investigative Firm or working directly for an insurance company in an SIU role, this manual will provide helpful hints and suggestions as you work your routine case load.

As a lifelong Private Investigator, John Bilyk is devoted to the claims investigations industry, teaching, writing and training. He has trained hundreds of investigators who have made Private Investigations their career.

Please look for Mr. Bilyk's newest book, "Case In Point. This book provides insight into working as a Private Investigator. The stories about Mr. Bilyk's encounters are not only entertaining but informative as well.

"The decision to become a Private Investigator was a life-long dream and an overwhelmingly satisfying career. I hope you too can enjoy the same success and wish you the best in your endeavor".

John C. Bilyk Jr., CFE

www.ingramcontent.com/pod-product-compliance
Lightning Source LLC
Chambersburg PA
CBHW081421230426
43668CB00016B/2315